THE HOLY SPIRIT AND POWER

THE HOLY SPIRIT
AND POWER
The Catholic Charismatic Renewal

KILIAN McDONNELL, O.S.B.
EDITOR

DOUBLEDAY & COMPANY, INC.
GARDEN CITY, NEW YORK
1975

Grateful acknowledgment is given for permission to quote material from the following sources:

The Documents of Vatican II, Walter M. Abbott, S.J., editor. Reprinted with permission of *America,* 1966. All Rights Reserved. © 1966 by America Press, 106 West 56th Street, New York, N.Y. 10019; *Life in the Spirit Team Manual,* published 1973 by Charismatic Renewal Services; *Roots of Ritual* by James D. Shaughnessy, 1973, William B. Eerdmans Publishing Co., used by permission; *As the Spirit Leads Us,* Kevin and Dorothy Ranaghan, 1971, Paulist Press. Copyright © 1971 by The Missionary Society of St. Paul the Apostle in the State of New York.

Library of Congress Cataloging in Publication Data
Main entry under title:

The Holy Spirit and power.

Includes bibliographical references.
1. Pentecostalism.   I. McDonnell, Kilian.
BX2350.57.H64   262′.001
ISBN 0-385-09909-6
Library of Congress Catalog Card Number 74-32573

Contents

Kilian McDonnell Preface   7

Heribert Mühlen The Person of the Holy Spirit   11

Herbert Schneider Baptism in the Holy Spirit in the
New Testament   35

Kilian McDonnell The Holy Spirit and Christian
Initiation   57

Ralph Martin Baptism in the Holy Spirit:
Pastoral Implications   91

Heribert Mühlen The Charismatic Renewal as
Experience   107

Francis A. Sullivan The Ecclesiological Context of the
Charismatic Renewal   119

Kevin Ranaghan Liturgy and Charisms   139

Donald Gelpi Ecumenical Problems and Possibilities   173

Preface

At a press conference following the Institute of Spirituality, held in St. Paul, Minnesota, in 1974, Father Louis Bouyer, the French theologian, expressed the opinion that the charismatic movement is the most important renewal movement in the contemporary Church. Avery Dulles, speaking to a group of Catholics preparing for the National Workshop for Christian Unity, in Charleston, South Carolina, early in 1974, said that as the "movement grows and feeds back into the Church on all levels, it may be expected to make a major contribution to the revitalization of Christianity in our time." The growth of the renewal at the international level, the large lay involvement as well as the growing participation of bishops and now a cardinal, makes it obvious that the renewal is not concerned with what is marginal and peripheral to the life of the Church in a sociological sense.

In a theological sense it touches what is central to the gospel and to the mystery of the Church. The renewal raises substantive theological issues. The present volume of essays is an attempt to clarify some of these issues at the level of serious theological reflection but in a language which is nontechnical.

KILIAN MCDONNELL

THE HOLY SPIRIT AND POWER

THE HOLY SPIRIT AND POWER

The Person of the Holy Spirit

HERIBERT MÜHLEN

At the outset of this anthology we wish to set down some theological considerations on the person of the Holy Spirit within the Holy Trinity. Then in a later essay of this volume ("The Charismatic Renewal as Experience") ecclesiastical questions will be discussed in greater detail.

What do we understand by the word "God?" What comes spontaneously to mind when we hear this term? Most likely the answer will be: *Father.* Or perhaps even more emphatically: the *Super Father,* who transcends the world and to whom we pray. What is sure, however, is that the word "God" does not lead us *in the first place to think of the Holy Spirit.* This discloses a quite fundamental deficiency of our conscious faith and of our piety. I would like to pose a second question. What are our non-reasoned and immediate thoughts when we hear the word "Holy Spirit?" This question too would probably yield but scanty results. Perhaps we recall that the Spirit is supposed to be the power which underlies all witness. We have received him in baptism and confirmation. Or possibly we are reminded of the Creed: I believe in the Holy Spirit and the holy Catholic Church. But if we reflect on the real impact of these expressions on our life and faith we will be forced to admit that we don't possess a very clear idea at all of what is meant by them. Who of us would care to say that he was filled with the Holy Spirit, as the adherents of the primitive Church without exception were able to assert. If we consider Paul's accounts of worship in the apostolic Church, then it becomes clear that the experience of the Spirit has something to do with the *social* experience of God. Every Christian has received his gift of the Spirit in order to contribute to the upbuilding of the community (1 Cor 12:11; 1 Pt 4:10, etc.). If an uninitiated or unbeliever comes into the assembly, and the sight of everyone speaking in prophecy stirs his conscience he will exclaim: "Truly *God is among you*" (1 Cor 14:25). The first Christians called this God within and among us the "Holy Spirit." Thus, God is not only the Creator who is *above* us and who exists *before* us (the first cause, the uncreated cause of evolution). He is also *within and among* us so that we are indeed able to see and hear something of him as we observe and hear other people offering themselves to God in praise through the power of the Holy Spirit (cf. Acts 2:33). In the following we will attempt to show that this one-sided and narrow understanding of God as the almighty Father, the absolute being, is in historical terms more or less coming to an end, and that experience of the Spirit of God similar to that which prevailed in the early Church would undoubtedly lead to a renewal of the Church and of theology. The historical period in which we live and which is now drawing to a close is so broad and extensive that it is necessary to reach far back into history in order to discover its roots. Vatican II says: "The human race today is poised at the beginning of a new age" ("Pastoral Constitution on the Church in the Modern World," Art. 4f.; 54). We have attempted elsewhere to elaborate what is meant by this statement.[1] Our purpose here after (1) commenting briefly on the narrowness of the traditional doctrine on God is to endeavor to describe the reality of the Holy Spirit in three mutually interrelated steps: the Holy Spirit (2) as the dynamic underlying a grace-filled fascination, (3) as the divine We, and (4) as the divine self-surrender.

THE NARROWNESS OF THE TRADITIONAL
TEACHING ON GOD

In his Summa Theologica, St. Thomas Aquinas has noted that the doctrine of the Holy Spirit suffers from a poverty of terminology. He is called love, but this word, according to Thomas, does not convey the distinction of the Spirit from the Father and the Son, since after all God by his very nature is love (Sth q. 37a, 1c). Elsewhere he says that the relationship of the Holy Spirit to the Father and Son and vice versa is "unnamed" because the words "Father" and "Son" in themselves characterize persons who stand in relationship one to the other. But use of the term "Holy Spirit," says St. Thomas, does not mean that one is to understand thereby a *person* in contradistinction to the Father and Son nor does it intend to express something about the *unique elements* of the relationship of this Spirit to the Father and the Son (Comp. theol. c. 59).[2] Is the reason for this lack of terminology and concrete imagery with regard to the Holy Spirit to be found in the nature of the Trinity itself, that is to say, in the fundamental inexpressibility of the divine nature or does it not also lie in the fact that in western tradition the articulation of the theology of God is too one-sided. Particular analogies have been emphasized in which the specific nature of the Holy Spirit as a person is excluded from the outset. It is, of course, obvious that any analogy is by its nature one-sided. Furthermore, analogies could be multiplied endlessly without being able to express fully the ineffable mystery. On the other hand, it is not possible for us to eliminate every comparison to our human experience when we speak of God. Even the Bible does this when it refers to God as Father, Son, and Spirit. However, the specific character of the relationship between these three divine persons is set forth in only the most rudimentary fashion. As a result, the historical process of understanding God's revelation in history relies heavily on a further elaboration of the biblical ideas. The dogmatic tradition has accomplished this in a very particular way, namely, by reference to the self-realization of the human spirit. But this reference is so thoroughly conditioned and restricted by history that the doctrine of the Holy Spirit has for all practical purposes become superfluous. In fact, we could easily fashion our entire theology without the doctrine of the Holy Spirit. This doctrine is almost inevitably seen as a pious addition, an edifying ornament, but never as the most basic proposition of the teaching on God. It is for that reason, for example, that according to the classic scholastic definition grace is viewed as a "participation in the divine *nature*." The indwelling of the Holy Spirit is seen only as a consequence of this fact. It is true, of course, that the *experience* of the living God has always been deeper and broader than the traditional *teaching* about God. Yet, it seems correct to say that this teaching on God, heavily influenced by the Deism of the seventeenth and eighteenth centuries, has come to an epoch-making conclusion in the middle of the twentieth century. The so-called God-is-dead theology is proof of this. Let us then begin by asking what analogies and images have been used in an effort to describe the relationship between Father, Son, and Spirit.

Leading the list is the experience of self as described above all by Augustine. It is based on Gn 1:26: "Let us make man according to our own image . . . And God created man according to his image, according to God's image he created him." According to the scholastic interpretation man's function as an image of God is related above all to God's knowing and loving himself.[3] Proceeding from this biblical text St. Augustine, and following him St. Thomas Aquinas, elaborated a broad analysis of human self-realization. The human spirit knows himself and in knowing himself he engenders in himself his own word, namely, himself. This knowledge of self leads then to love of self, and thus the spirit through his own will produces his own self loving himself. Thomas Aquinas then continues very characteristically: We are not aware of any additional process within the human spirit; rather in these two processes the spirit returns to itself as in a circle. In God this circle is absolutely closed. God is absolutely related to himself and as such also brings all created things into relationship to himself (De potentia, q. 9, a. 9; cf. Summa contra gentiles, IV, 26). In knowing himself in his Logos, in his word, and in loving himself God is turned back *absolutely* and in an incomprehensible manner in upon himself. God is, therefore, the absolute being, the *absolute person*. In fact, St. Thomas carries this interpretation so far that he says that this absolute divine personality could have become man. According to him it is possible to abstract from three divine persons and consider the nature of God itself as something personal. One could say then that this could have become man (Sth III, q. 3, a. 3).[4] Thus, it is clear that the system of scholastic theology is quite able to exist without the mystery of the Trinity, and the same is true of the entire traditional theology of God. Indeed, even the Incarnation can be described without it.

An important criticism must, however, be introduced at this point: Why does St. Thomas and the entire tradition refer only to the first half-verse of Gn 1:27? The entire verse reads, of course: "And God made man according to his image and likeness, according to the image of God he created him, *man and woman he created them!*" We are confronted here with a quite surprising statement, one that has hardly been given adequate attention. Genesis insists that the image of God is *man and woman*; in no way is it exclusively and solely a single person who relates to himself in self-knowledge and self-love. There has never been a serious attempt to apply the relationship between man and woman or the family to our understanding of the divine life. What is the reason for this?

Thomas explains very clearly. He says flatly: "It must, of course, be noted that the physical engendering of human life takes place through an active and a passive force. The active force is called father and the passive mother . . . It pertains to the father to bestow upon the offspring his nature and to the mother, on the other hand, to receive and to give birth. Thus, she is passive and receptive. However, the Word is engendered through God's knowing himself, a process which is not passive but is, as it were, active. Furthermore, the divine Spirit does not stand in a relationship of potency to anything, but it is always in act. Because of this the generation of the Divine Word does not in any way involve the maternal principle but only the paternal" (Summa contra gentiles, IV, 11). Because of a particular metaphysical theory of knowledge the relationship between father and mother is *not* proposed *explicitly* as an analogy designed to illustrate the mystery of the Trinity; it is rather positively *excluded*. Not only does this manifest a deficient understanding of human progeneration as such, as though the father alone were the active principle; far more fundamentally it represents a one-sidedly paternal understanding of being. This point must now be investigated a bit more in detail. In what follows I am relying on a number of essays by Franz K. Mayer[5] in which he attempts to show that from the very beginning western metaphysics has progressively eliminated maternal experiences of being.

In order to be able to understand this process it is necessary to journey far back into intellectual and religious history. For the pre-Socratic philosophers and the Ionian natural philosophers nature was still seen as the great mother, the "earth mother." In this view, being and becoming were, it is true, in a polarity relationship; yet they were not disjoined in a dualistic fashion. The great mother is one who engenders and gives birth to herself; she is her own becoming.[6] This is the reason why in the language of myth the symbol of the great mother always appeared in the closest possible relation to the experience of time and fate, of change and becoming. The masculine principle of the "great father," on the other hand, was associated with the conquest of time and fate. It is therefore appropriate to distinguish between the maternal and paternal experience of being. Thus, Plato in his dialogue Timaios 50C still compares the genuine reality of the idea with the "father" symbol. The boundless depths of matter are related to the "mother" symbol. For him matter is "an invisible, formless, all-embracing reality, difficult to grasp, sharing in some incomprehensible way in the realm of ideas" (Timaios 51A). All created things, that is, the visible world, constitute a composite of the idea viewed as a paternal principle and of limitless matter seen as the maternal principle. The same distinction can also be found in Aristotle when he characterizes sex as a mirroring of matter and form (Metaphysics 988a). Prime matter analogically related to the feminine principle and form analogically related to the masculine principle are the ontological basis for the origin of all things. Aristotle, in fact, explicitly compares prime matter (that is, pure potency, free of any determined form) to a "mother" (Physics 192a).

This restricted understanding of the maternal experience of being, its undervaluation as compared to the paternal, has, of course, also influenced the manner in which God is understood. According to classical Greek ontology things possess a greater degree of form and *energeia* the less they share in prime matter. It is for that reason that the first and highest being, the divine Being, must be understood as pure *eidos*, pure form and pure *energeia* without any relationship whatever to prime matter.

Thus, Scholasticism characterizes God as pure act. Any notion of *apeiron*, of the undetermined, the boundless, is categorically excluded. A final reason why the God of the philosophers is unhistorical emerges at this point. It is not possible for him to become. There is in him no *potentia*; he is radically alone; he is related totally and absolutely to himself. Since both the ancient and medieval systems of thought viewed the feminine, maternal principle as passive and receptive—in other words, potential—Thomas was forced by the logic of his system to eliminate any maternal aspect of being from his analogical description of the divine life. But in the process certain basic biblical passages are far too narrowly interpreted or indeed completely ignored. One need only recall that already in the Old Testament the Spirit acted as God's power within history. It is by virtue of the Spirit that God is present among his people. The God of the Bible not only exists in and unto himself; he also goes out beyond himself; he acts upon the history of men even to the extent of becoming fully involved in it. This occurs precisely through that *dynamis*, that power, which is called Pneuma.

The growing intellectualization of the understanding of God was accompanied by an extensive intellectualization of faith itself. The scholastic distinction between *ratio* and *affectus* is evidence of that. Already in Plato the nonrational aspects of human existence, above all the affections and the emotions, are identified with the feminine principle. "Spirit" is equated with human "masculinity," with discursive reason, and with the objectifying functions of the human spirit. As a result, the experience of being is transformed into active, wide-ranging *experience of things*, and the effective and emotional depths of the human act of faith become completely obscured. The second Council of Orange had declared against the Semipelagians that faith *began* with the emotion of faith, *through* which we are led to believe in Christ.

This emotion of faith, the Council affirms, is produced in us through the working of the Holy Spirit in us, and it is this that leads us to baptism (DS 375). The suppression of the emotional level of faith is clearly visible today in its historical consequences. The rationalization of faith has turned God into a "Supreme Being" whose existence can only be ascertained through a rational process based on the fact of creation. But he can't really be "experienced," something Kant believed he could prove. In the contemporary crisis facing all the Christian churches it is also a matter of the highest concern that this emotional level of faith be revived. Sometime in his life the adult Christian must acquire a deep personal involvement (cf. Acts 2:37). He must let himself be made Christian on the deepest level of his emotions through the working of the Holy Spirit. But where are the emotions of most Christians? Do they really love God *with their whole heart?* Or are they not rather completely absorbed in the manifold fascinations of our modern culture? Faith is neither a pure act of reason nor is it a pure act of the will. It is rather an act of the whole person including the emotions. It goes without saying, of course, that a distorted emphasis on the emotions is equally erroneous, for it leads to sentimentality. Nevertheless, the complete rejection of the emotional level of faith because of some rational "enlightenment" has no basis in the New Testament. A reversal of this process is a historical necessity at this time.

There are certain hopeful signs in this connection in the charismatic movement. It is, therefore, perhaps not completely accidental that the feminine element is preponderant in this movement; at least it was so in the beginning. Women seem to be more receptive to it. (Jesus, too, after his resurrection, bestowed his first appearances on women.) It has taken hold in religious orders of women. In our modern western culture a man is really permitted to express only *one* emotion: aggression and anger. Receptivity, openness, surrender, on the other hand, are considered "feminine." The image of the ideal man is the Western hero, and so it is not entirely inappropriate to speak of a "John Wayne syndrome." But this has led to a suppression and rejection of other emotions, and it produces either neuroses or a focusing of all one's emotional forces into aggression. The charismatic renewal will be able to institute radical corrective measures in this regard. This movement, therefore, not only represents the beginning of a truly *trinitarian* approach to our understanding of God, but also and precisely because of this it will help heal our human culture from the wounds of historically conditioned distortions and exaggerations.

THE HOLY SPIRIT AS THE DYNAMIC OF
A GRACE-FILLED FASCINATION

a) *God is not only present to himself; he also reaches beyond himself.*

We are now no longer concerned about the legitimacy of the distinction between the paternal and maternal experience of being; we simply affirm that a deeply moving experience which comes from the outside, being caught up with something and the ecstasy that follows—none of this is considered by the classic Metaphysics as pertaining to the essential characteristics of being. The classical transcendentals—truth, unity, goodness, beauty—are derived through the analysis of human introspection. In this framework everything mysterious, every centrifugal tendency, everything that takes hold of a person or that impels a person out of himself is an abomination. There is simply no place in such a system for man's experience of himself beyond himself. The nature or essence of any being is rooted in the immutable, constant, enduring present. Time, becoming, the passive involvement with something—these have to be overcome through rational thought. Yet the experience of God as it takes place in the Bible reveals a God who is outside of himself, who surrenders himself, who pours himself out. It is only in this context that we will be able to understand the biblical utterances concerning the Spirit of God. It would be possible to summarize as follows: *The Spirit of God is God himself insofar as he breaks out of himself and goes beyond himself.*[7] Accordingly, the Spirit of God within us is the one who sweeps us along to Jesus, who propels us into the boundless depths of God. This experience of being outside of oneself has nothing to do initially with enthusiasm or a particular form of ecstasy in which a person is no longer in control of himself. It only means that the experience of the Spirit does not lock a person into a radical turning inward. It rather breaks through this radical inward-looking tendency precisely so that one can be with Jesus or with God.

It is particularly important to stress this in view of the fact that according to 1 Tm 6:16 the Father dwells in inaccessible light; no one has ever seen him nor will anyone see him. According to Jn 5:38, we are not able to hear the voice of God nor can we see his *eidos*, his form. There is in God no outline, no form, which we can grasp and comprehend in the sense that the ancient philosophies understood it. Rather, he has appeared in bodily form in Christ. Yet, he is no longer with us in the form of this particular man either; he has gone away. What has remained is that Spirit within us, of which it is said that he has been sent into our hearts (Gal 4:6).

The Spirit of God is, so to say, the reality of God dwelling within us. This reality is nearer to us than we are able to be to ourselves and as such carries us on to the inaccessible light in which the Father dwells. But before we attempt to describe this in greater detail it is necessary to delve into manifestations within our contemporary culture of living outside of oneself, of fascination. This will enable us to integrate the biblical statements into our own existential experience.

b) *Fascination and religious experience*

We are using the rather worn-out term "experience" in the same sense in which the Bible uses the word "heart," e.g. Acts 2:37. After St. Peter's Pentecost sermon there is this reference to those who heard his words: "They were pierced to the heart and said to Peter and the other apostles: What should we do, brothers?" In this context "heart" refers to that center of each person's being, the complex of all his physical and spiritual forces.[8] This center, therefore, these innermost depths, are "pierced" by the message of Jesus. And it is into this heart too that the Holy Spirit is sent.

Thus, it is not an intellectual experience that is meant in this context, nor is it purely interior, an *a priori* or transcendental experience. It is, rather, a personal encounter and involvement with the person of Jesus. There are always two aspects to this encounter: fear and joy (or withdrawal and attraction), as we are about to show. When we are caught up in these two aspects simultaneously we talk of fascination. For the moment we will define this term simply as an involvement with an *extraordinary reality which withdraws even as it exercises an inexplicable attraction.* Fascination is neither a superficial enthusiasm, on the one hand, nor is it a thoroughgoing fear of death. Rather it always occurs when something draws us onward *precisely as* it withdraws from us. It is because something or someone withdraws into an unattainable sphere that we are drawn onward. We are now able to describe this phenomenon in our modern culture in broad outline and to prove that every person, provided he is mentally healthy, is fascinated by something or someone.

The opposite of fascination is boredom, which consists essentially in the sadness experienced when nothing attracts us anymore, nothing fascinates us any longer. This could be demonstrated by considering the fascination with anything brand-new in modern technology, with the utter newness of the first moon expedition, the first heart transplant, etc. What is involved here is a kind of crossing into new frontiers, a liberation from oneself through a level of being that goes beyond oneself. A similar manifestation can be observed in modern sports. The rarity of a world-record-breaking high jump, for example, so fascinates people that they are reduced to breathless silence as they watch. The same phenomenon is found above all in modern hero worshiping. The political leader is still perceived today as a kind of savior who is going to free his people for an ever higher standard of living and limitless material development. This same kind of fascination is associated with beauty queens, popular singers, film stars, etc. However, it is present above all in a love relationship. It is precisely here that the dialectic between attraction and withdrawal is probably experienced most intensely. In an interpersonal encounter attraction (closeness) and withdrawal (differentness) are not two mutually exclusive occurrences. They are two reciprocally developing aspects of one and the same occurrence, in short, of fascination. It will not be possible here to elaborate on this thesis; we wish merely to make the following brief points.[9]

1. Fascination is a fundamental human experience which pertains to human existence as such.

2. This experience is characterized by the dialectic between attraction and withdrawal, between closeness and differentness. The thing evoking this fascination attracts the other by withdrawing.

3. Fascination is a contrast experience from a twofold point of view. a) The object of my fascination always approaches me from a point outside of me. b) Normally it is not the daily, customary, but rather the non-daily, the extraordinary, the special.

4. For the most part we become truly involved only when something or someone *continually* fascinates us. In that case that which fascinates us is often invested with the brilliance of an absolute and ultimate value, as is clearly evident in the modern cult of the hero. The object of the fascination has the tendency to appear unassailable, liable neither to being questioned nor to being doubted.

c) *Fascination which Jesus brought into the world*

The gospel accounts of encounters with Jesus invariably show that people were deeply struck by him. His person and his works evoked fear and joy *at the same time*. Of course, one must remember that these pre-Resurrection accounts, above all the miracle stories, are colored by the Easter glory of the Risen Lord. But there is no need here to develop this point in any more detail. It is pre-eminently the Resurrection itself that produced "fear and great joy" in the women (Mt 28:8). Here joyful enthusiasm was joined with simultaneous and deeply felt emotions of fear. The biblical writers see this same fascination taking place at the time of the birth of Jesus: "The splendor of the Lord shown about the shepherds and they were greatly afraid. But the angel spoke to them: Do not fear, for I announce to you a great joy" (Lk

2:9). And between the Nativity and the Resurrection is that long series of incidents, events, and impressions which portray Jesus during his "public" life as a fascinating man. Even when he was twelve years old the Bible could report of him: "Everyone who heard him was amazed at his understanding and answers" (Lk 2:47). In connection with his account of the healing of the man possessed by a dumb spirit Matthew asserts: "Everybody was astonished and said, *we have never seen the like of that*" (9:33). The reason for the astonishment is not the cure as such, but rather the unusualness of this event.[10] Similar things can be observed in the other miracle accounts (cf. Mt 12:23; Mk 2:12; 5:41f.; 6:51). People are overwhelmed and astonished by the words of Jesus, too (Mt 7:28; 13:54; 19:25; Mk 1:22; 6:2; 7:37; 11:18; Lk 4:32; 9:43).

The fascination which Jesus brought into the world is most clearly evident in the New Testament reinterpretation of the temple idea. In the time of Jesus the temple of Jerusalem with its Holy Place and the Holy of Holies was without question a place set aside. Here God was present in a special way.

This place was attractive and terrifying at the same time, for the high priest was permitted to enter the Holy of Holies only once each year. A vast array of ritual prescriptions safeguarded the sacredness of this event. The temple was the source of enduring fascination. Of course, Jesus, too, clearly looked on the temple as the "house of God" and the location of a special divine presence (Mt 12:4; Lk 6:4). Nevertheless, the teaching and person of Jesus are "more than the temple" (Mt 12:6). John associates the incident of the cleansing of the temple with words of Jesus going back to the earliest tradition: "Destroy this temple and in three days I will build it up again" (Jn 2:19). With his post-Easter perspective he applied these words to the "temple of his body" (2:21). We can conclude from this that Jesus in his person and being represents the fulfillment and therefore the end of the Old Testament temple cult. It is Jesus who is from now on the actual and the most proper locus of the presence of God. And it is from here that divine fascination emanates.

It was only slowly that this transformation of the God-experience (so difficult for the Jewish mentality to comprehend and indeed the basic reason why Jesus was condemned) penetrated into the early Christian consciousness. The early Church is perfectly aware of the newness of her Pneuma experience, but she finds it hard to articulate. Finally, Paul puts it into words: "The temple of God is holy and this temple you are" (1 Cor 3:16). "Or do you not know that your body (which always means 'you') is a temple of the Holy Spirit who dwells within you" (1 Cor 7:19). This means that for the primitive Church it is no longer the temple of Jerusalem with its Holy Place and the Holy of Holies which is the primary focus for encounter with God and fascination. Rather, it is the community itself in its mutual and reciprocal pneumatic existence. From this it is clear to what extent Christian fraternal relationships mediate the experience with God. In the Old Testament a neighbor is simply a person with whom one shares a common allegiance to God and his laws. Interpersonal relationships are hardly ever explicitly related to the special character of the covenant bond. At any rate, it is never explicitly stated in the Old Testament that the people communicate the experience of God, the divine fascination, *to each other*. It would never have occurred to them to look for an encounter with the God of the covenant in their mutual relationships.

In the light of the New Testament, however, it must be affirmed that *the Pneuma is that grace-filled and life-giving fascination in which Christians encounter each other. It is the incorporeal reality which makes possible a physical experience of God*. Every individual Christian is that "portion" (=*temenos*—temple), in which the Doxa, the glory of God, appears in its mysterious future state. Every Christian, every neighbor, stands apart from everyone else and therefore draws and withdraws at the same time. Yet, this fascination is not a superficial attraction; it is always achieved through the cross, for the cross of Jesus in John's Gospel is at the same time his glory. His glory emerges from his death. This pneumatic fascination is filtered through the cross, for the sensory preoccupation of man generally prevents the spirit living within us from really becoming manifest (cf. Cor 12:7). Nor is this fascination any mere casual feeling of good will; it is judged by its actual effect on one's life: "I was hungry and you did not give me anything to eat" etc. (Mt 25:41).

It is clear, therefore, that not every fascination is associated with Jesus of Nazareth, with the grace of God. Jesus himself, who is present in man through his Pneuma, is the primary component of pneumatic fascination. 1 Cor 12:1–3 shows this very clearly. Paul seeks to explain the essence of the gifts of the Spirit to the Corinthians by referring to the fascination familiar to them from their pagan cults: "You know how you were drawn to dumb idols when you were still pagans." Being caught up by an overpowering force—in other words, fascination—is described here by Paul as a general human experience and is recognized as such. The power by which the pagans were drawn is "mute," of course, and anonymous, whereas the criterion for judging the existence of the sway of the Spirit (pneumatic fascination) and its nature is expressed in the proclamation "Jesus is Lord" (v. 3). Pneumatic fascination, therefore, means *to experience Jesus*. This takes place not only when one makes some charitable offering (St. Paul stresses in 2 Cor 8:5 that such donations are given first of all to the Lord and only secondarily to one's fellow Christians) but also and above all in the ancient worship service which Paul describes as a "revelation of the Spirit" (1 Cor 12:7). The many different gifts of the Spirit alive in the Church in their reciprocal relationship constitute "the Christ" (1 Cor 12:12); they make up the body of Christ as it is revealed in the local community.

THE HOLY SPIRIT AS THE DIVINE WE

We have already shown toward the end of the second section that the pneumatic fascination is always associated with the experience of community and church. According to 1 Cor 12:11 the one Holy Spirit provides for a variety of gifts precisely in order that he might appear as the One. It is the constant and invariable testimony of the New Testament that the Pneuma, unlike the *ruach* Jahve in the Old Testament, is never given to one person alone. The *ruach* was certainly given to a specific judge, an individual king or prophet. In the New Testament, however, the Pneuma of God or of Jesus always comes to the many at once. Luke illustrates this in the image of the *one* firestorm which came to all who were assembled in the same place. Therefore, the Holy Spirit is never exclusively "mine" or "yours" but rather "our" Spirit! It is true, of course, that each one receives him according to his own capacity (1 Cor 12:11; cf. Acts 2:3), but it is always with reference to the others, to the entire body of Christ. In this way the one Holy Spirit creates a grace-filled *unity* among the many. We have already shown that fascination is not something that happens exclusively within a person; it is no isolated, purely interior experience. It rather always touches people from the outside and is aroused most intensely through other people. It is inconceivable apart from the experience of oneness in a community. Thus, St. Paul, in connection with his description of the multiplicity of gifts of the Spirit which come from the one and the same Spirit, says: "In the *one* Spirit *we were all*—Jew and Greek, slave and free—brought to the one body and we were all nourished with the *one* Spirit" (1 Cor 12:13). This "we all" can only be understood in the light of the one same Spirit dwelling in the many. The central pneumatic experience of the early Church always involves the experience of a grace-filled *We*. There is no exception to this fact in the New Testament, not even with respect to those who have been given the task of leadership. The declaration of the so-called apostolic council of Jerusalem is couched in these famous words: "The Holy Spirit and *we* have decided not to impose any further burden on you" (Acts 15:28). It would have been unthinkable for James or even Peter to have said: "The Holy Spirit and *I* have decided."

It is in this context that a great deal of light is shed on certain expressions of Jesus in the we form. First of all, there is absolutely no record in the New Testament of Jesus joining with other men in the use of "we" when he is speaking to his Father. In his relationship to God he never places himself on the side of the rest of mankind. "It is true that according to Matthew Jesus taught his disciples to pray: 'Our Father.' But nowhere in the synoptics, not even in the most ancient sources, did he join with his disciples in such an 'our.' "[11] In St. John, too, this manner of speaking occupies a central place. After the Resurrection Jesus says to Mary Magdalene: "But go to my brethren and tell them: I am going to *my* Father and *your* Father, to *my* God and to *your* God" (Jn 20:17). The expression "our Father" does not occur at all in St. John. Those expressions of Jesus in which he uses "we" are related to the Father and show an absolute exclusiveness. Thus, they also express something of his divine relationship with the Father.

This is most apparent in the Johannine writings. The "We" in Jn 10:30: "I and the Father are one," or Jn 17:22: "*We* are one," refers to a marvelous unity with the Father which is manifested as an exclusive, two-sided "We." First, it appears as an exclusive I-Thou relationship: "All should be one; as You, Father, in me and I in You, all should be one in *us*" (Jn 17:21). The Johannine Christ is speaking to the Father and reveals his relationship to him in the personal pronouns "I" and "Thou." This divine I-Thou becomes a "We" when related to the totality of the disciples in a "We-You" relationship: they should be *one* in *us!* The exclusive We in this relationship between the two divine persons is meant to be made present in the multiple We of all of the disciples of Jesus! This sheds great light on the words of Jn 14:23: "If someone loves me, he will keep my word and my Father will love him. *We* shall come to him and make our abode with him." This "We" is to be taken first of all in an exclusive sense: the Father and I. Yet, the coming of this dual We takes place through the enduring presence of the other Paraclete which is promised in this passage: "If you love me, you will keep my commandments; I will ask the Father and he will send you another Paraclete who will be with you always, the Spirit of truth which the world cannot receive" (Jn 14:15ff.). Now the Father *continues to live* in inaccessible light and no one has ever seen him (1 Jn 4:12); the Son too has returned to the Father. What remains with us forever (Jn 4:16) is the Spirit of Father and Son, that is to say, the divine We as such. It is possible to summarize as follows: *To experience the Spirit involves an encounter with the dual We of Father and Son and equally fundamentally an awareness of this divine presence within the multiple We of the disciples of Jesus.*

This analogy is solidly based on the thought patterns of the New Testament itself. To develop it further and to integrate it into our own existential development it will be necessary to examine in some greater detail the structure of the family as a "we-unit." It is not the human person in his exclusive interiority who is the image of God but rather the dual We of a man and a woman. This is already suggested by Gn 1:27 (if one wishes to apply this text at all). The scholastics continually used it but in a very one-sided and inadequate way. Obviously there is no question of this passage containing a trinitarian reference. Nevertheless, this text does serve as an essential corrective to the one-sided traditional interpretation. For the relationship of father, mother, and child is not merely to be understood as a helpful concept in clarifying a trinitarian model. It is entirely possible to see it as an expression and reflection of the mystery of the Trinity itself. Obviously, sexual, personal, and other differences must be discounted, for every attempt to speak of a feminine principle in God leads to philosophically untenable positions which have nothing to do with the doctrine of the Trinity itself but rather represent a gratuitous and uncritical "transfer" of human experiences to God. But when this relationship is *formalized* in the triad I-Thou-We it becomes remarkably expressive. Nor are the sexual aspects entirely eliminated; rather they are maintained for it is clear that the archetype of the I-Thou relationship is that of man and woman. A revealing analogy for the so-called generation of the Holy Spirit, which in dogmatic tradition is exclusively described as a *spiratio activa*, is found in the generation of the child from both parents. The child is never exclusively "mine" or "yours"; it is always "our" child, since it is produced neither from the father alone nor from the mother alone but rather in a single act of two persons. We refer to such joint actions as "we-acts." One never addresses another person with the pronoun "we" as one might use "you"; "we" is used rather when referring to something in conjunction with that other person. In we-acts persons either relate jointly to some third person or they produce it, as parents bring forth a child. If the Father is characterized as the divine "I" (this is emphatically the way the Old Testament looks at Jahve) and the Son as the divine "Thou," then the generation of the Holy Spirit can be seen as the strictly conjoined *we-act of the Godhead.* It is not possible at this juncture to do more than suggest that this provides a framework for understanding the bonds of marriage (specifically including the physical consummation) as an expression and reflection of the marvelously fecund divine act of life. There is a basis here for developing a theology of marriage based on the Pneuma, including a radically new articulation of the real meaning of marriage as a sacrament.[12]

THE HOLY SPIRIT AS THE DIVINE SELF-SURRENDER

We do not really arrive at the central core of Pneumatology until proceeding from an appreciation of the mystery of the cross we describe the Holy Spirit as the common self-gift of the I and the Thou. Pneumatic fascination and pneumatic experience of the We acquires its proper order and depth when each person's self-surrender to Jesus and through him to God is then expressed in a self-surrender to one's fellow men. God's reaching outside of himself is probably expressed the most clearly in Rom 8:32: "If he did not spare his own son but gave him (*parédoken*) up for all of us, how then can he not fail to give us everything with him?" The Father who shows us no *eidos,* no "form," no countenance reveals himself to us by giving up that which is most properly his, his son, for God so loved the world that he gave his only son (*édoken,* Jn 3, 16). Should not the Father also be affected by this? Indeed, the Father did not spare *himself* in giving up his own son for us! Here we have gone beyond the emotionless, passionless face of the platonic or aristotelian God who, serenely turned in on himself, is sufficient unto himself and who draws all things to himself without himself going out of himself. This God who did not spare himself is related to creation and to the people of the covenant in more than a merely logical relationship. There exists a true transpersonal relationship. But the Thou who has been given up has also given *himself* up for us to the Father (*parédoken heautón;* Eph 5:2,25; Gal 2:20) and has humbled himself (Phlm

2:7). This *parédoken* expressed twice by Father and by Son precisely because it is jointly uttered by Father *and* Son reveals to us as it were the essence of God's nature as manifested in salvation history.

The formal identity of the surrender is actually manifested in two completely distinct ways: The scriptures never say that the Father, the divine I, gives himself up; the reference is always to the Son. It is true that he did not spare *himself*, but he did not give himself up either. Rather he gave up that which was most properly his, his Son, his Thou. Thus Rom 8:32 suggests three aspects of this surrender, aspects which are neither interchangeable nor separable from each other. Not interchangeable: The one who is giving up is not identical with the one being given up; nor is he identical with his surrender. For it is no anonymous process of self-giving that does the surrendering but it is the Father, the divine I himself. Inseparable: Neither the one surrendering nor the one given up exists for himself in a fundamental isolation. For the one given up, the divine Thou, has no other existence than as someone who has been given up. The one surrendering, the Father, exists only as someone who surrenders. It is this reaching out of himself which constitutes the Father as a person, as a constant dogmatic tradition affirms. The Father according to this tradition is the *relatio paternitatis*; as a person he is the relationship of fatherhood as such. The process of self-giving certainly cannot be understood if it is considered in isolation. The same thing is true when applied to the Son: The one giving himself, the Son, the divine Thou, is not identical with the one to whom Jesus surrenders himself nor with the process of the surrender itself.

The New Testament frequently suggests that this process of Jesus' giving himself up to the Father involves the divine Pneuma in some way. According to Heb 9:14 Jesus presented himself to God "in the power of the eternal spirit."[13] If one examines the entire New Testament there can be no doubt whatever that this Pneuma in whose power Jesus surrendered himself to the Father is *identical* in the most proper sense of that word with the "Pneuma from God" (1 Cor 2:12). The Pneuma is God the Father in his reaching out beyond himself; thus he is that *one* process by which the Father gives up his Son and the Son gives himself to the Father. We may therefore attempt a third formulation: *The Pneuma is the single divine self-surrender itself.* In his first epistle St. John says the same thing in these words: God is love. This is how God showed his love for us. He sent his only Son into the world (4:8). He could just as well have said: God is self-surrender, for "we have come to know the love (of God) since he (Jesus) has given up his life for us" (1 Jn 3:16). Therefore, we can remain in him and he in us only in the measure that he has given us of his Spirit (1 Jn 4:13), that is to say, in the measure he has placed his own self-surrender into the depths of our hearts.

In conclusion, I would merely express this hope: Pneumatology was traditionally and in part still is today a more or less edifying part of the theology of God. But it is possible that our own days will witness a break-through to a new epoch in our experience of God where God will be approached not in the first place as the Creator-God who dwells blissfully *on high* in isolation but equally as the Holy Spirit who dwells *in us* and who reigns in our hearts. For the Holy Spirit is mentioned no less than Jesus and God the Father. Together with both of them he is adored and glorified. He speaks to us in the word of the Bible just as he does in the wordless words of our prayers. When we do not know what we should pray for, the divine self-surrender who rules within us carries us forward. He forces us out of ourselves so that our shriveled heart might transcend its craving to preserve this radical isolation and come to be with Jesus and through him with God. An *interior* renewal of the Church has to come about by recapturing that ancient fundamental experience which was the foundation of the early Church, and from which the powerful Constantinian Church was formed. Year by year we are gaining a deeper realization that this so-called Constantinian epoch with its far-reaching sacralization of power and of ecclesiastical office has come to an end. The pneumatic experience in this era was largely confined to the fascination emanating from those who held official rank in the

Church and who represented God before the people. Today, however, an experience has emerged in the charismatic pneumatic renewal which though preserving the past is modifying it so as to set the stage for the beginning of a new age.

FOOTNOTES

[1] Cf. H. Mühlen, "Der Beginn einer neuen Epoche der Geschichte des Glaubens," *Theologie und Glaube*, 64 (1974), pp. 28–45.

[2] Cf. Sth. I, 40, 4c; 36 1c. For a further discussion see H. Mühlen, *Der Heilige Geist als Person in der Trinität, bei der Inkarnation und beim Gnadenbund* (Münster i.W.,² 1968), pp. 3ff.

[3] For a more detailed analysis see H. Mühlen, *Der Heilige Geist als Person*, pp. 12f.

[4] *Op. cit.*, pp. 318ff.

[5] "Trinitätstheologie und theologische Anthropologie," *Zeitschrift für Theologie und Kirche*, 68 (1971), pp. 427–77; "Trinität und Familie in de Trinitate XII von Augustinus," in: *Revue des Études Augustiniennes*, 8 (1972), pp. 51–86; "Der aristotelische Gottesbeweis im Lichte der Religions-Geschichte," in: *Zeitschrift für Religions- und Geistesgeschichte*, 24 (1972), pp. 97–121.

[6] "Trinitätstheologie und theologische Anthropologie," p. 435.

[7] Cf. K. Stalder, *Das Werk des Geistes in der Heiligung bei Paulus* (Zürich, 1962), p. 47.

[8] Cf. Maxsein, LthK,² vol. V, p. 285f.

[9] Cf. our more extended analysis in *Entsakralisierung*, chapter I.

[10] Cf. Bertram, in: Kittel, *Theologisches Wörterbuch zum Neuen Testament*, vol. III, pp. 36, 42.

[11] Cf. Schrenk, in: Kittel, *Theologisches Wörterbuch zum Neuen Testament*, vol. V, 988, p. 16; cf. H. Mühlen, *Der Heilige Geist als Person*, pp. 95–99.

[12] Cf. H. Mühlen, *Entsakralisierung* (Paderborn,² 1971), pp. 505–26; ibid., *Ehe als Dienst, Lebendiges Zeugnis*, October 1973, pp. 5–18.

[13] Cf. H. Mühlen, *Una mystica Persona. Die Kirche als das Mysterium der heilsgeschichtlichen Identität des Heiligen Geistes in Christus und den Christen: Eine Person in vielen Personen* (Paderborn,³ 1968), pp. 273ff.

Baptism in the Holy Spirit
in the New Testament

HERBERT SCHNEIDER, S.J.

The expression "baptism in (with) the Holy Spirit" or "Spirit-baptism" names the central religious experience of the Pentecostal churches that trace their origin back to Topeka, Kansas, or Azusa Street in Los Angeles at the turn of the century. It names also the central experience of the various neo-Pentecostal groups in the various historic Protestant churches and of the Catholic charismatic renewal. Without going into details about the teaching of the above-named groups, one can say that Spirit-baptism gives the individual a new relationship with God, the Father, and that this relationship is brought about by God.[1] From the Pentecostal teachings and even more from the personal testimonies to Spirit-baptism the content of this new relationship seems to be twofold: 1. It is an experience of being accepted and personally loved by the Father. 2. It is an empowering by the Spirit to do what Jesus did. The purpose of it is the establishment and upbuilding of the Body of Christ in, with, and through Jesus to the glory of the Father.

All Pentecostal groups draw the interpretation and understanding of the religious experience of Spirit-baptism from the New Testament: what happened to Peter and the other disciples at Pentecost and to all the early Christians is happening to me also. The following pages, therefore, are concerned with Spirit-baptism in the New Testament. We will first consider the Book of Acts, then the Pauline Letters, and finally the gospels. In Acts and

Paul we will investigate first the language used to describe this experience, then the contexts, the circumstances of it, and finally the signs, which mark it authentic in these books of the New Testament.

It is clear that the wealth of material and the limited space available will limit the extent of our discussion. Even so it is hoped that this will contribute to a better understanding of Spirit-baptism from the New Testament standpoint.

SPIRIT-BAPTISM IN THE BOOK OF ACTS

The Language Used:

We notice right away that the New Testament does not use the expression "baptism in (with) the Holy Spirit" or "Spirit-baptism." These expressions developed within the Pentecostal groups and became their fixed technical terms to refer to the experience in question. The closest New Testament term is "baptised (with) in the Holy Spirit." John the Baptist prophesies in Mark's Gospel: "One stronger than I will come after me . . . I baptize you with water, he will baptize you in the Holy Spirit" (Mk 1:7–8 par.). In the Book of Acts the same prophecy is put in the mouth of Jesus. He tells his apostles not to leave Jerusalem until they have received the promise of the Father, about which he had spoken to them. Jesus continues: "John baptized in water, you will be baptized with the Holy Spirit within a few days" (Acts 1:5; cf. also Acts 11:16). The author of the Book of Acts considers the Pentecost event (Acts 2:1–13) and the "conversion" of the household of Cornelius (Acts 10:1ff.) fulfillments of this prophecy of John/Jesus. This is clear from Acts 1:5 and 11:15–16.

Although Acts understands the Pentecost event and the conversion of Cornelius as the fulfillment of Jesus' promise of Spirit-baptism, yet chapters 2 and 10 of Acts do not use this term. A variety of other expressions are used instead. We want to list them and add in parenthesis other sections of Acts, where the same expressions occur.[2]

The Promise

| Acts 1:5 | "to be baptized with the Holy Spirit" | (11:16) |
| 1:8 | "the coming of the Holy Spirit (upon)" | (19:6) |

Pentecost and Cornelius

2:4	"to be filled with the Holy Spirit"	(9:17; 13:9, 52; 4:8, 31)
2:17, 18, 33; 10:45	"to pour out the Spirit"	
2:38; 10:47	"to receive the Holy Spirit"	(8:15, 17, 19; 19:2)
10:44	"the Holy Spirit fell down on"	(8:16; 11:15)
	"to give the Holy Spirit"	(5:32; 8:18) (11:17; 15;8)[3]

From the above we see that there is no fixed terminology in the Book of Acts. All seven expressions are used within the context of the Pentecost event and the conversion of Cornelius, if you take it together with the promise of the Spirit in Acts 1:5,8. All seven expressions describe the same event. They are interchangeable. The most used expressions in Acts are "to be filled with the Holy Spirit," "to pour out the Holy Spirit," "to receive the Holy Spirit," "the Holy Spirit falls upon."

If we look at the texts in parenthesis, we find that from the language and also from the context (as will become clear below), the following are considered "Spirit-baptisms" along with the Pentecost event and the conversion of Cornelius (Acts 2; 10:1–11:18): the conversion of Samaria (8:4–24; esp. 14–17); the conversion of Paul (9:1–19); the baptism and the reception of the Spirit of the disciples at Ephesus (19:1–6).

The Context of Spirit-baptism in Acts:

Leaving chapter 2 of Acts aside for the moment, all the other four episodes are similar in that they describe the initiation of an individual or a group into the community of the Lord Jesus. The gift of the Spirit marks the initiation process as completed. In the cases of the Samaritans, Cornelius, and the disciples at Ephesus, the gift of the Spirit is something that can be "seen and heard."[4] The outward manifestation is not only the proof that the Spirit has really been given, it is also the sign that this person is really a member of Jesus' people (8:5–16; 10:47 and 11:15,18; 19:1–6). The gift of the Holy Spirit given in a way that can be "seen and heard" is the authenticating mark of the members of the new community that started with the group in the Upper Room. It is the bond of their unity. Baptism is an essential part of the initiation and intimately connected with the gift of the Spirit.[5] What is true of the above episodes is also true of Paul's conversion. The gift of the Spirit marks also his "christianization" complete.[6]

In Acts the gift of the Spirit marks the entrance of a person into the community of Jesus. The Spirit makes a man a Christian. He is the bond of unity among the various local communities. This gift is not something hidden, but something that can be noticed. In fact, in the Book of Acts it would be true to say that, where there is no experiential manifestation of the Spirit, there the Spirit had not been bestowed.[7]

Content and Meaning of the Experience:

Since all the other episodes refer back to the Jerusalem community, we must now turn to chapter 2 of Acts to discover the meaning of the gift of the Spirit for Luke and the Church he wrote for. Chapter 2 is divided by Luke into three parts: 1) the Pentecost event, 2:1–13; 2) Peter's sermon about the meaning of the Pentecost event, 2:14–40; 3) the Christian community, 2:41–47.

Acts 2:1–13: The Pentecost Event:

The key verse is verse 4 taken together with the second half of verse 11. In verse 4 Luke states: "All were filled with the Holy Spirit" and as sign of being filled with the Holy Spirit "they began to speak in other languages as the Spirit prompted them to speak." The content of their speech was praise of the great deeds of God (v. 11b). The coming of the Spirit meant for them a "realization" that Jesus really was Messiah and Lord (2:33 as Peter will explain). They experienced the love of God and knew that they were saved and acceptable to God. They realized that this was not just for them but for all men who would turn to God through Jesus. Praise of God, therefore, became the first sign and expression of the coming of the Spirit. The gift of praise made them a "eucharistic" community, a community characterized by giving thanks to God.[8]

The other details of the Pentecost narration are ways of Luke to explain more clearly the meaning of this event. The Holy Spirit fills them on the Jewish feast of Pentecost. This feast celebrated at the time of Christ at least in priestly circles the covenant of Sinai.[9] Luke probably wants to suggest through the gift of the Spirit on Pentecost that God is now initiating the new covenant. The noise of the wind, tongues as of fire, and even the then known world represented by the groups from the various countries mentioned, all these details seem to be connected in some way with the Sinai event: the making of the covenant and the gift of the law. We cannot be sure, because our closest parallels to Luke's account come from rabbinic traditions which are much younger than the Pentecost narrative in Acts.[10] From Peter's sermon, better from his quote of Jl 3:1–5, we know that Luke wants this gift of the Spirit to be understood as the eschatological, final, and universal outpouring of the Spirit.

To summarize then: The Spirit is given to all disciples without exception. Through it they experience the reality of their salvation and God's saving power for all men through Jesus. They break out in enthusiastic praise of God's saving deed in and through Jesus, who has been revealed to them by the Spirit indeed as Lord and Messiah (2:33).

Peter's Sermon, 2:14–40:

Luke makes Peter stand up and address the crowd, explaining the true meaning of the event just witnessed. Luke wants the talk understood as inspired by the Holy Spirit just as much as the praise of God in tongues. The same Greek verb describes both.[11]

In his talk Peter makes three assertions and proves them from scripture according to the custom of the times. He asserts, first of all, that what the people witnessed is the final, permanent out-pouring of the Spirit of God on all mankind (2:16). Thus the age of salvation has begun and the sign of it is the possession of the Spirit. Peter's proof is the text from Jl 3:1–5 (Acts 2:17–21). Next Peter states that God raised Jesus from the dead. His proof-text is Ps 16:8–11 (Acts 2:25–28). The Father gave the Spirit to Jesus. Jesus poured the Spirit on his disciples as the crowd is "see-ing and hearing." Ps 110:1 (Acts 2:34–35) is the proof for the ex-altation of Jesus. Thus Jesus is really Lord and Messiah. Peter makes clear that the Spirit comes from the Father to them through Jesus. The Spirit, the possession of both Father and Jesus, is poured out on the disciples. The connection of the Spirit to Jesus had not been clear from the Pentecost event (Acts 2:1–13) alone.

A word is in order on the method of argumentation in the talk of Peter. He starts with the event that the people witness. He then states his interpretation of the event and says it is true because it had been foretold and foreordained in scripture as his quotes prove. Finally he returns to the experience of the disciples and himself, saying that Jesus is Lord and Messiah, because the Spirit has really been poured out. The experience is so real that it can be "seen and heard." Arguing in this way from scripture was con-vincing to the people at that time with a Jewish background.

Finally asked by his hearers what they should do, Peter tells them the requirements for sharing in the same gift of God: 1) repentance (turning to God), 2) baptism in the name of Jesus (accepting him as Messiah and Lord) for the forgiveness of sins, and 3) reception of the gift of the Spirit. A large number accepted the message and are baptized (Acts 2:41).

The Christian Community:

Luke ends chapter 2 with a description of the community. He wants this community understood as the work and gift of the Spirit in spite of the fact that the Holy Spirit is not mentioned in this final section of chapter 2. Whenever Luke describes a mani-festation of the Spirit in the first five chapters of Acts, he always describes it in terms of the community of believers, as if to say this is the result of the Spirit's presence.

In chapter 4 the assembly prays for a new outpouring of the Spirit, in order to proclaim the gospel with courage (4:24ff., esp. vv. 29–30 and 31). Verse 32 describes the result of the prayer in terms of the community. The beginning of chapter 5 narrates the punishment of Ananias and Sapphira through the Holy Spirit. Again this manifestation is followed by a description of the community of the faithful (5:11–16). Here, however, the emphasis is exclusively on the healing ministry. Perhaps Acts 9:31 and 16:5 are other examples of this.

The Signs of Authentic Spirit-baptism in Acts:

Of course, we must realize that Acts, or for that matter the rest of the New Testament, never poses the explicit question what are the signs of authentic Spirit-baptism. And yet from what Acts describes as the work of the Spirit, we can come to an idea of what constitutes authentic Spirit-baptism for the Lucan Church.

In Acts 1:5 Jesus promises that his disciples will be baptized with the Holy Spirit in a few days. They will receive power to be witnesses (Acts 1:8). The promise is fulfilled on Pentecost day and they do receive the power to witness that Jesus is Messiah and Lord (Acts 2:3ff.) through praise and preaching (Acts 2:4b,11b; 2:14ff.). Peter speaks without fear before the Sanhedrin (compare Acts 4:7 with Lk 20:2; Mt 10:20 and Acts 1:8; 4:29–31; 5:32,41,42). The apostles can't be made to keep quiet. This same courage to witness is demanded from and presupposed in the deacons (6:3). Stephen is all this (6:5). His opponents cannot get the better of him, because the Holy Spirit is with him (6:10 and again Lk 20:2; Mt 10:20). One thing must be noted, however: official proclamation of the Good News of Jesus, the Lord, seems to be entrusted by the Spirit not just to every member in the community, but to the leaders, to the apostles.

Miracles support the proclamation of the Good News (2:43). The apostles heal the sick and free the possessed (5:12,16; compare Mk 6:56; Lk 4:40–41). In fact the apostles do what Jesus did through the Spirit. The healing ministry however, contrary to preaching, is not reserved to the apostles alone. Stephen (6:8), Philip (8:6,13), and Paul, who in Acts is not considered an apostle, heal and free people through the power of the Spirit (14:8ff.; 20:9ff.). Paul himself is cured of his blindness by Ananias (9:18ff.).

The most important authenticating mark of the coming of the Spirit is really the community of Jesus. The members are obedient to the teaching of the leaders of the community (the apostles) (2:42; 4:33). They share everything they are and have. They are brothers (2:44; 4:32,34,35). They pray as a community and share meals in simplicity and joy (2:46). God makes the community grow (2:46–47; 5:12b–14). God works miracles, i.e. he heals and frees people (5:12,15,16; 2:43; 4:33). Thus the community of Jesus, i.e. the community of people who share in the Spirit of Jesus, is characterized by unity, joy, sharing of life and goods, community prayer of praise and thanks, miracles and growth. These are the signs for the Book of Acts that the Spirit is really present, and consequently that they are really the community of the end time, the true people of God.

We see then that Acts does accent and stress the power of the Spirit present through miracles, prophecy, and tongues. The Spirit's experiential presence is the fact that spreads the faith. In the last analysis, however, Luke sees the most important sign of the presence of the Spirit in the lives of the Christians with each other in obedience to the apostles and in a sharing of their persons and goods in joy, simplicity, and prayer.

SPIRIT-BAPTISM IN THE PAULINE LETTERS

We shall follow here the same procedure as above. First, we shall list Paul's expression for the experience of the Spirit, then we shall investigate the context and the meaning of the gift of the Spirit.

Paul's Language:

1 Thes 4:7,8	"God continually gives us the Holy Spirit"
Rom 5:5; 2 Cor 1:22	"The Holy Spirit, which has been given to us"
2 Cor 5:5	"God, the giver of the pledge of the Spirit"
Gal 3:2,14; Rom 8:15	"To receive the Spirit"
1 Cor 6:19	"You have the Holy Spirit from God"
2 Cor 1:22; Eph 1:13–14; 4:30	"You were sealed with the Holy Spirit"
Gal 4:6	"God sent the Spirit of his Son into our hearts"
1 Cor 12:13	"In one Spirit we were all baptized into one body"
1 Cor 12:13	"We have all been given to drink of the one Spirit"
1 Cor 6:11	"You were cleansed, made holy, and justified in the Name of the Lord Jesus and in the Spirit of our God"
Ti 3:5	"We were saved through the bath of regeneration and a new creation of the Holy Spirit"

We notice again that Paul also has no fixed terminology, when referring to the reception of the Spirit. All the above are interchangeable. This does not deny that the different expressions emphasize different nuances of the meaning of the gift of the Spirit. All are metaphors trying to come to grips with this event in the believer's life. Paul, too, has a preference. When he focuses on God, he uses more often than not the verb "to give" (cf. 1 Thes 4:8; Rom 5:5; 2 Cor 1:22, 5:5) and when speaking of us, he uses very often simply "to receive" (cf. Gal 3:2,14; Rom 8:15; 1 Cor 2:12). Also the image of being sealed in the Spirit is frequently used (Eph 1:13–14, 4:30; 2 Cor 1:22). Paul does not use the expression "to be baptized with or in the Holy Spirit" as it is used in Acts. 1 Cor 12:13 emphasizes entrance into the Church, baptism through the instrumentality of the Spirit. He wants to stress the unity Christians have in the Spirit. It could be that Paul is referring in this verse to the two basic sacraments of baptism and the Eucharist.[12]

Another important fact can be gleaned just from the consideration of Paul's language. He usually speaks of the reception of the Spirit as a single past event in a Christian's life. He expresses this through the use of the Aorist tense of the Greek verbs (cf. 1 Cor 2:12, 6:11; 2 Cor 1:22; Eph 1:13–14, 4:30; Gal 4:6; Rom 8:15; 1 Cor 12:13; and Ti 3:5).

Context and Content:

All the texts we found, where Paul talks about the gift of the Spirit, refer in one way or another to the event that makes a man a Christian: namely his turning in faith to Jesus, accepting baptism and consequently receiving the Spirit.[13] We turn now to the different texts.

The Gift of the Spirit and Life:

In 1 Thes 4:1–8, especially in verse 8, Paul refers to Ez 36:27 and 37:14.[14] Paul changes the future tense of the promise in Ezechiel to the present tense of fulfillment. Now, at this moment, the Spirit is continuously being given. It is thus that the Spirit gives new life and the power to live according to God's will (1 Thes 4:8). The change from a life of sin to one of holiness that takes place at Christian initiation is achieved by the creative power of the Spirit. Paul describes this activity of the Spirit as cleansing, making holy, justifying (1 Cor 6:11). We belong to God through the Spirit (1 Cor 6:19; cf. also Eph 4:4–6 and 30). Paul's call to a life according to God's will is motivated precisely by recalling the gift of the Holy Spirit. He is the foundation of the Christian life.

The Gift of the Spirit and Hope:

The hope of the Christian was founded when the love of God was poured out in his heart through the Spirit (Rom 5:5). Paul uses the perfect tense of "to pour out" to show that the gift was

given at a particular point of time in the past and is still being
given now in the present. The verb itself is the same as that used
by Jl 3:1 (cf. Acts 2:17,18,33; 10:45). The foundation of our
hope is the experience of God's love and what this love can do
in us. God's love becomes ours. This love that opens us radically
to other men is the first and foremost charism, gift of the Spirit
(cf. also 2 Cor 5:5; Eph 1:13–14).[15]

The Gift of the Spirit and Sonship:

The Galatians experienced the presence of the Spirit of God as
a consequence of their faith in Jesus. They became new people
through the gift of the Spirit (Gal 3:2–5). The Spirit is the gift
of salvation and the experience of the presence of the Spirit is the
"proof" of acceptance of God. It marks the existence of the son
of God (Gal 3:14).

The Spirit makes us sons. This spells out more what justification means. To be son does not just mean to have one's sins for-
given, but describes a new relationship to God marked by love
and trust. The gift of the Spirit of Jesus is the "proof" of it (Gal
4:6). The result of the gift of the Spirit of the Son is the ability
to pray and live "Abba-Father" (Gal 4:6). Paul stresses the role
of faith. He stresses further that the Spirit is given to each individual. It is not simply the collective experience of the believing
community.[16]

The Spirit's first gift is prayer for Paul just as much as for Acts.
In Gal 4:6 and Rom 8:15 he enables us to pray "Abba-Father."
This is further enlarged in Rom 8:26–27. Man cannot pray. Only
the Spirit of God can give a man this ability. Prayer is the sign of
sonship.

The Marks of Spirit-baptism in Paul:

For Paul just as much as for Acts, baptism and the gift of the
Spirit belong together. The gift of the Spirit marks the beginning
of a new relationship of an individual with God (Gal 3:1–5:14;
2 Cor 1:21–22; Gal 4:6; Rom 8:15). Something happens to a man
then. The gift of the Spirit is not a thing. It is dynamic, it is life
itself. It is a power continuously given, an ongoing relationship

with God (Ti 3:4–7; I Thes 4:8). It founds the ability to live according to God's will. It enables us to respond to God in the prayer of a son (Gal 4:6; Rom 8:15,26,27). The unity among Christians, loyalty toward one another, the hope of final fulfillment, and the ability to serve rests on the now-experience of the Spirit's power within us (Eph 4:4–6; 2 Cor 1:21; 1 Cor 12:13).

If we compare Paul with Acts, we notice at once that Paul stresses that the Spirit of Jesus is the beginning and end of Christian life. We would miss the point completely, if we thought Paul equated the possession of the Spirit simply with the ability to keep the commandments. The Spirit of Jesus changes our very mode of existence. The love of God himself becomes our act of existence. Therefore, love and the qualities that flow from it are the marks of the baptism of the Holy Spirit for Paul.[17] This very same love is the power for service in the community. The charisms are nothing but the love of God poured into our hearts, become visible now in specific services in the community: calling the community together, turning her more fully to the Lord, building her up as the people of praise God called in and through Jesus (Eph 1:14).

On the other hand, Paul sees in a life lived only for oneself a sign of the absence of the Spirit of God. The various sin catalogues express this insight. Paul sees this most exemplified in the sexual perversion of the society he lived in on the one hand and in the inability of people to praise and thank God on the other (Rom 1:21ff., for example).

In the Book of Acts, the Spirit is the missionary force of the Church. He reveals Jesus and gives the gift of praise and thus forms the eucharistic community. Luke talks in terms of this community marked by obedience, prayer and sharing of everything in joy, when he wants to show the effects of the Spirit. Paul sees deeper and simply sees the Spirit as the foundation of all aspects of Christian life. The Spirit reveals Jesus. He lets us experience our new relationship to God. This issues in the gift of praise, "Abba-Father."[18] The charismatic manifestations of the Spirit are just as important and essential for Paul as they are in the Book of Acts.[19] In both, the gift of the Spirit is a conscious experience of a new relationship with God through Jesus manifested in and through the ability to love the brothers with the very life-giving power of God himself. For both this process starts with the hearing and accepting of the gospel in faith and obedience, followed by self-surrender to Jesus openly in the Church in baptism and receiving as a mark and sign of acceptance by God the Spirit of sonship. The new Christian is thus made capable by God of joining the community of sons.[20]

THE GOSPELS

The gospels do not deal with the Christian initiation as directly as Paul does, for example, in his letters to the various communities. They do not describe the development and spread of the Church through the Spirit as does the Book of Acts. The gospels center on the words and deeds of Jesus, who fulfills his task through the power of God's spirit. Jesus is described by the synoptic gospels as a charismatic. The early Church seems to have understood its own charismatic endowment as the power of continuing the work of Jesus. We, therefore, want to look at the baptism of Jesus, his preaching about the Kingdom of God and his deeds in order to understand this connection more clearly.

The Baptism of Jesus (Mk 1:9–11 *par.*):
Actually the baptism of Jesus by John does not occupy the center of interest. The gospels are much more interested in the descent of the Spirit on Jesus after the baptism. There are many details in this narration that exegetes are still struggling to understand. Clear seem to be that in Mark, the oldest form of narration, three events are stressed that are attempts to express really one and the same reality: 1) Heaven is ripped open and the contact between men and God is re-established in Jesus. 2) The Spirit of God descends on Jesus. 3) The voice proclaims Jesus as son on whom God's favor rests. The Spirit of God is the bond of unity with God and the closeness of this unity is described in terms of a father-son relationship. Finally as Son and endowed

with the power of the Father, Jesus goes out to do battle with the devil and is victorious.

We have here in this short narrative at the very beginning of the public life of Jesus a kind of summary of the entire task of Jesus, described in the rest of the gospel namely, to free man for God by defeating the forces of evil through the power of God.

Luke wants Jesus' ministry understood as directed by the Spirit (Lk 4:14). Jesus himself refers to his charismatic ministry in Matthew and Luke, when asked by John's messengers, whether he is the one expected (Mt 11:2ff., esp. v. 5; Lk 7:18–23, esp. 21–22; cf. also Lk 4:18ff.). In all gospels Jesus is accused of working through the power of the devil (cf. Mk 3:22; Mt 12:24; Lk 11:15; Jn 8:48). Jesus rejects this accusation. In the first three gospels he asserts that in experiencing the power of God by being healed and freed the hearers are, in fact, experiencing the kingdom of God (cf. Mt 12:28; Lk 11:20). Jesus equates his healings and exorcisms through the power of God with the coming of the kingdom.[21] This understanding of equating the kingdom of God with the presence of the power of God seems to be behind an alternate reading of the petition "Your kingdom come" in the Lucan Our Father which reads: "Your Holy Spirit come upon us and cleanse us."[22]

Jesus gives his disciples and apostles the power to preach, heal, and exorcise (Mk 3:13ff. esp. v. 14; Mt 10:1,7,8; Lk 9:1,2; 10:9,17, 19; compare with Mk 6:12,13; Lk 9:6). The longer ending of the Gospel of Mark (16:9–20) sees the charismatic gifts of driving out demons, tongues, immunity from poison, and healing as signs that will accompany the preaching and acceptance of the gospel in faith. Here the same basic gifts of the Lord of the Church, namely, healing, deliverance, and preaching become the gifts of those who belong to Jesus. Perhaps the promise contained in the late ending of the Gospel of Matthew refers to something similar. Jesus will be with his community always (Mt 28:20).[23]

In the Gospel of John the main function of the Spirit is the glorification of Jesus. For John this means that the Spirit reveals the meaning of the death and resurrection of Jesus for the believer. Thus for John the first gift of the Spirit is the power to forgive sins (Jn 20:21–23). The Spirit grants a new relationship to God (Jn 1:12–13) in the sense that everything that Jesus is and brings is now realized in the believer. Through the gift of the Spirit Jesus is now present in his community (cf. Jn 10:10; 15:11; 4:10–14; 7:37–38; and 6:63).

The Spirit has a second function in this gospel, which is expressed especially in the paraclete sayings found in the Last Supper Discourse (Jn 14–17). The paraclete "teaches" the community and convicts the world in its rejection of God and his son Jesus. He teaches and recalls Jesus (Jn 14:26). He leads them in understanding God's salvific work in and through Jesus (Jn 16:13). He gives courage to witness (Jn 15:26–27). The Spirit is behind the preaching of the gospel (Jn 16:13 and 1 Jn 1:3,5).[24] The work of the paraclete in John corresponds approximately to the charisms of wisdom, teaching, knowledge, and prophecy or again to the charismatic ministry of apostles, teachers, and prophets in Paul (compare 1 Cor 12:8ff.; Rom 12:6ff.; and esp. Eph 4:11ff.).

For John baptism in the Holy Spirit and the "sacrament of baptism" are one and the same event. Presupposed is faith in Jesus. Faith brings men into a new relationship with God first and foremost through the forgiveness of sins (Jn 3:3,5). In the community of the faithful the Spirit manifests Jesus in his salvific work, i.e. as Jesus who is glorified and exalted in his death on the cross. John emphasizes above all the revelatory function of the Spirit.

The teaching on the Spirit we find in the four gospels is fundamentally the same as found in the Book of Acts or in Paul. Here, too, we find the realization that through Jesus the believer is granted a new relationship with the Father. In the gospels the charismatic endowment of the Church is understood to come from the same source as the charismatic endowment of Jesus, namely, from the Spirit of God. Christian existence is a continuation of the work and mission of Jesus in the world and the basis for this is the charismatic presence of the Spirit of Jesus in the early Church. The Christians could do and actually did the same deeds as Jesus: the Good News was preached with power and this power manifested itself in healing and deliverance. The Spirit of God thus made them really the Body of Christ; Christ in the world today. For the gospels just as much as for Paul and Acts the gift of the Spirit of the Lord alone makes a man a Christian. The gift was understood to be authentic, when it enabled the individual and the community to continue the mission of Jesus in power.

SUMMARY AND CONCLUSION

From the above survey of the New Testament teaching on Spirit-baptism, we can say that the New Testament does not have a fixed terminology referring to the gift of the Spirit. "To be baptized in the Holy Spirit" is one expression among many and by no means the most frequently used. It is natural that as time goes on different churches develop different fixed terminologies. This happened in the post-apostolic churches, where such terms as "illumination" and "sealing" became technical terms for the sacrament of initiation.[25] The Pentecostal churches and charismatic groups of today have a fixed expression, a technical term, referring to the experience of the person and power of the Holy Spirit, namely "baptism of the Holy Spirit" or "Spirit-baptism." Substituting other New Testament expressions from Acts or Paul to avoid confusion with the sacrament of baptism does not really help, because all the other terms, too, refer to the first gift of the Spirit at Christian initiation. The expression "to be filled with the Holy Spirit" is ambiguously used in Acts: it names both the first coming of the Spirit (2:4; 9:17) and a subsequent strengthening for a particular task (4:8,31; 13:9); or consolation received (13:52).

The witness of the New Testament is unanimous that to be a Christian means to have been given the gift of the Holy Spirit. A Christian is a person who has been anointed with the Spirit of Jesus (Mk 1:9ff. par.; Gal 4:6; Rom 8:15). In other words, hearing the gospel, accepting Jesus as Lord and Messiah, acknowledging one's faith in Jesus before the Church in baptism and receiving the gift of the Spirit together form the one whole experience of becoming a Christian for the New Testament churches.[26]

For the New Testament the Spirit of God is never given in such a way that it cannot be experienced. If the Spirit cannot be "seen and heard" it has not been given (Acts 8:16, for example). For the synoptic gospels the gift of the Spirit manifests itself in the power to do what Jesus did. Where people are healed and freed from evil, there the gospel becomes really Good News, there God is present in power and his kingdom is now among us. The Book of Acts also stresses healing and deliverance. Again the apostles do what Jesus did (Acts 5:12,16 and Mk 6:56; Lk 4:40–41). In addition, Acts stresses the gift of praise (Acts 2:4b and 11b, etc.) and the gift of brotherhood (Acts 2:42ff., etc.). The Spirit is the power behind the growth of the Church. Paul emphasizes the gift of the Spirit as the foundation of the Christian life. The Spirit opens a person and makes him capable of loving others. This love-existence, which is always God's gift (Rom 5:5), becomes visible in the various services (charisms) for the up-building of the Church (1 Cor 12:3). The gift of praise stands in first place (Gal 4:6; Rom 8:16; 26–28) followed by all the others mentioned in Rom 12:6ff.; 1 Cor 12–14; and Eph 4:11ff. It is precisely the power and presence of the Spirit become visible in the community in service that transubstantiates a group of people into the Body of Christ. The New Testament Church is a charismatic Church.

For Paul the purpose of the gift of the Spirit is unity. He expresses it through the image of the Body of which Jesus is the head (Lord) and we are members (1 Cor 12:13ff.; cf. also Eph 1:14). The Book of Acts pictures the Church as a community of obedience and total sharing of person and possessions, whose common existence is characterized by simplicity, joy, praise of the Father, and growth. The ultimate sign of the presence of the Spirit for Paul and Luke in Acts is therefore, the community of the people of Jesus assembled under his lordship, united in brotherhood through the power of his love for the praise of the

Father. The presence of the Spirit fulfills the prayer of the Lord before he died:

> I pray . . . that all may be one as you, Father, are in me, and I in you; I pray that they may be one in us, that the world may believe that you sent me. (Jn 17:20–21)

FOOTNOTES

[1] Stephen B. Clark, *Baptized in the Spirit* (Pecos, 1970), p. 47.

[2] James D. G. Dunn, *Baptism in the Holy Spirit* (London, 1970), pp. 70ff.

[3] Peter reports to the Council of Jerusalem that the pagans had received the very same gift as the apostles at Pentecost.

[4] Cf. Acts 2:33: Peter, talking about the gift of the Spirit refers to what the crowd sees and hears. Simon, the Magician, offers money for the power to confer the Spirit, Acts 8:18,19; Tongues mark the falling of the Spirit on the household of Cornelius, 10:46; and on the Ephesian disciples, 19:6.

[5] In each case where baptism and the gift of the Spirit are separated, it seems that Luke's theological motives are the cause of the separation. In Samaria and in Ephesus Luke seems to want to show that only within the believing community of Jesus is the Spirit given. Cf. H. Conzelmann, *Die Apostelgeschichte* (Tübingen, 1963), p. 55; E. Haenchen, *Die Apostelgeschichte* (Göttingen,[10] 1956), p. 265; A Loisy, *Les Actes des Apôtres* (Paris, 1920), p. 368; H. Schlier, "Die Einheit der Kirche im NT," *Exegetische Aufsätze und Vorträge* (Freiburg, Basel, Wien, 1964), p. 182; E. Käsemann, "The Disciples of John the Baptist in Ephesus," *Essays on New Testament Themes* (London,[3] 1968), pp. 144, 146. Cornelius' case is made to show concretely that God wants the pagans in the Church without them having to accept Judaism first. Cf. M. Dibelius, *Aufsätze zur Apostelgeschichte*, ed. H. Greeven (Göttingen, 1951), p. 105.

[6] Does Paul's gift of tongues date back to this time? Cf. 1 Cor 14:18.

[7] Cf. Acts 8:16, e.g.

[8] Most of the important commentaries both old and new see in v. 4 the key pronouncement of Acts 2:1–13. Cf., e.g., the commentaries of Ambrose, Augustine, Leo, and Cornelius a Lapide; among more modern commentaries cf. Bauernfeind and the study of N. Adler, *Das Erste Christliche Pfingstfest Sinn und Bedeutung des*

Pfingstberichtes APG 2, 1–13 (Münster, 1938), pp. 66–67. For the meaning of the gift of tongues as a gift of praise consult: P. Brunner, "Das Pfingstereignis: Eine dogmatische Beleuchtung seiner historischen Problematic," *Volk Gottes, Festgabe für Josef Höfer,* ed. Heimo Dolch (Freiburg, Basel, Wien, 1967), p. 240.

[9] Cf. B. Noack, "The Day of Pentecost in Jubilees, Qumran and Acts," *Annual of the Swedish Theological Institute* 1 (1962), 88. An important study for the understanding of the Jewish background of the feast of Pentecost is J. Potin, "La fête juive de la Pentecôte," Vol. I and II (Paris, 1971).

[10] N. Adler, *Das Erste Christliche Pfingstfest,* pp. 53, 57, 61.

[11] Compare "Apophthegomai" in v. 4 and v. 14.

[12] This is at least the view of H. Lietzmann, *An die Korinther,* I and II (Tübingen,[4] 1949), p. 63, and H. H. Wendland, *Die Briefe an die Korinther* (Göttingen,[8] 1962), p. 69.

[13] Cf. G. R. Beasley-Murray, *Baptism in the New Testament* (London, 1963), p. 275.

[14] Paul uses the Greek text of the Old Testament.

[15] C. H. Dodd, *The Epistle of Paul to the Romans* (London, 1954), p. 74: "The meaning of this very fundamental statement is not simply that we become more aware that God loves us, but that in the same experience in which we receive a deep and undeniable assurance of his love for us, that love becomes the central motive of our own moral being."

[16] Rom 8:15. 14–17 is a more developed parallel to Gal 4:6.

[17] Compare the lists of the qualities of love in 1 Cor 13 and Gal 5:22ff.: patience, gentleness, respect for the brothers, honesty, service, and purity, etc.

[18] In his article "Der gottesdienstliche Schrei nach der Freiheit," BZNW 30 (1964), 226, Käsemann interprets the prayer of the "Abba-Father" as charismatic prayer of the community worshiping together. The same is stated in the commentaries of the letter to the Romans of O. Holtzmann, p. 651; Lietzmann, p. 86, and Althaus, p. 236. J. Schniewind interprets it as a manifestation of the experience of being justified in his essay "Das Seufzen des Geistes, Röm. 8, 26.27," *Nachgelassene Reden und Aufsätze,* ed. E. Kähler (Berlin, 1952), pp. 91–93.

[19] G. Hasenhüttl, *Charisma, Ordnungsprinzip der Kirche* (Freiburg, Basel, Wien, 1969), p. 235. Cf. here Gal 3:1–5, where the charismatic manifestation proves Paul's point.

[20] Gal 4:6 and Rom 8:15.

[21] James D. G. Dunn, "Spirit and Kingdom," *Expository Times* 82 (1970), pp. 37ff.; G. R. Beasley-Murray, "Jesus and the Spirit," *Mélanges Beda Rigaux* (Gembloux, 1970), pp. 468ff.; S. S. Smalley, "Spirit, Kingdom and Prayer in Luke-Acts," *Novum Testamentum* 15 (1973), pp. 59–71.

[22] Cf. K. Aland, *The Greek New Testament* (London, 1966), under Lk 11:2.

[23] E. Windisch, "Jesus und der Geist," *Studies in Early Christianity*, ed. J. Case (London, New York, 1928), pp. 227 and 229. Windisch emphasizes the continuity between Jesus and the Spirit-filled early Church. Cf. also R. Otto, *Reich Gottes und Menschensohn. Ein Religionsgeschichtlicher Versuch* (München, 1940), p. 277: "the early traditions describe Christ as a charismatic. We say: this description is authentic, because only in this way can you explain his historical influence issuing in a pneumatic-enthusiastic community."

[24] Compare F. Mussner, "Die johanneischen Parakletsprüche und die apostolische Tradition," *Biblische Zeitschrift* 5 (1961), pp. 59ff., and R. E. Brown, *The Gospel According to John*, vol. I and II (Garden City, N.Y., 1966 and 1970), p. 1135.

[25] F. H. Kettler, "Taufe, III Dogmengeschichtlich," *RGG* VI,[3] 1962, pp. 638, 641.

[26] This is the conclusion of the book of James D. G. Dunn, *Baptism in the Holy Spirit*, op. cit., pp. 228–29. Cf. also H. Schlier, *Der Brief an die Epheser* (Düsseldorf,[4] 1963), p. 70.

The Holy Spirit and Christian
Initiation

KILIAN MCDONNELL, O.S.B.

In approaching the theological problem at hand general areas will
be discussed: the broad theological context of the renewal, the objections of Yves Congar, the relation of the imparting of the
Spirit to the celebration of initiation, and the specificity of the
charismatic renewal.

I would like to set the renewal within its broad theological context by posing some questions about its specificity. One of the
major theological problems for those who view the charismatic
renewal from the outside is its specificity, those special concerns
of the charismatic renewal. An exaggerated doctrine of the Holy
Spirit, to the point where Christ seems to be set aside and the
Spirit placed in the center of one's religious consciousness, seems
to the outsider to be one element of specificity in the charismatic
renewal. The renewal seems to take on a special character because
of its attention to the gifts of the Spirit, including those not a
part of normal Church life, namely, prophecy, speaking in
tongues, healing, interpretation. These particular gifts seem to
form the specificity of the charismatic renewal. The renewal also
seems to be distinguished by its concern for experience of presence
at the level of consciousness, a new dimension of religious awareness. The role that experience plays in the charismatic renewal
appears to define the Christian life in terms of a series of peak experiences, where the believer moves from religious experience to
religious experience, from mountaintop to mountaintop. In this

sense the specificity of the renewal appears to be a species of pneumatic triumphalism.

There are a number of reasons why the specificity of the renewal gets out of focus. Though the renewal sees itself as a renewal of the whole Church, lay and cleric, the renewal is largely lay in character. That is, it is lay in the modalities of its expression, in its procedures, in the immediacy with which it approaches religious reality, in the lack of nuance in its theological expression. In political terms one would say that it is a populist movement. In no sense is this lay character of the renewal to be deplored; rather, it is one of its great strengths and is to be guarded and cherished as such. Because populist movements tend to construct an ideology which is clear, simple, well-defined, and unyielding, the theological basis of the charismatic renewal is sometimes presented as an ideology, that is, in a manner which is clear, simplistic, narrow, and unyielding. If a theological evaluation is made at the level of its populist expression, then the judgment on the renewal may be severe. Here, however, as in judgments upon any populist renewal in the Church, judgment should be made not on the basis of its least acceptable theological expression, but on the basis of its more mature expression.

BROAD THEOLOGICAL CONTEXT OF THE RENEWAL

As Donald Gelpi has pointed out, the renewal at its best is consciously trinitarian.[1] Since the charismatic movement generally sees the theological locus of the baptism in the Holy Spirit in the celebration of initiation (baptism, confirmation, Eucharist), it represents a renewal of baptismal consciousness and realities, with all that that means for insertion into the trinitarian life. The renewal makes its own the teaching of Vatican II on the reappropriation of those trinitarian elements which define the Church. "By an utterly free and mysterious decree of His own wisdom and goodness, the eternal Father created the whole world . . . He planned to assemble in the holy Church all those who would believe in Christ."[2] "The Son, therefore, came on mission from his Father

. . . To carry out the will of the Father, Christ inaugurated the kingdom of heaven on earth and revealed to us the mystery of the Father . . . The Church, or, in other words, the kingdom of Christ now present in mystery, grows visibly in the world through the power of God."[3] *The Constitution on the Church* then goes on to speak of the role of the Holy Spirit in the constituting of the Church. Pentecost plays a decisive role in the sanctification of the Church and in providing access to the Father through the one Spirit. Then the *Constitution* continues to detail the role of the Spirit in the life of the Church. Mention is made of the same Spirit dwelling in the Church and in the hearts of the faithful. "In them he prays and bears witness to the fact that they are adopted sons (cf. Gal 4:6; Rom 8:15–16 and 26)."[4] The document speaks of the role of the Spirit in relation to truth and to the ministerial gifts. "The Spirit guides the Church into the fullness of truth (cf. Jn 16:13) and gives her a unity of fellowship and service. He furnishes and directs her with various gifts, both hierarchical and charismatic, and adorns her with the fruits of his grace (cf. Eph 4:11–12; 1 Cor 12:4; Gal 5:22)."[5] Finally, the text alludes to the Spirit as the source of the Church's life and the reason why she possesses that persistent and surprising source within her for renewal. "By the power of the gospel he makes the Church grow, perpetually renews her, and leads her to perfect union with her Spouse."[6]

Within this pronounced trinitarian ecclesiology the *Constitution* develops the doctrine of the people of God's participation in the prophetic office of Christ. "The body of the faithful as a whole, anointed as they are by the Holy One (cf. Jn 1:20,27), cannot err in matters of belief."[7] From the prophetic office of the people in God in general the Council proceeds to talk about charisms in particular. The Council recognizes that the Holy Spirit who acts in the sacraments and in the "Church ministries" also sanctifies and leads the people of God. The Fathers of the Council wished to repeat the doctrine of St. Paul that no Christian is without a charism: "Allotting his gifts 'to everyone according as he will' (1 Cor 12:11), he distributes special graces among the faithful of every rank."[8] The charisms are recognized not as personal adornments, benefiting only the recipient, but as ministries to the whole Church, instruments of renewal and upbuilding. "By these gifts He makes them fit and ready to undertake the various tasks or offices advantageous for the renewal and upbuilding of the church, according to the words of the apostle, 'The manifestation of the Spirit is given to everyone for profit' (1 Cor 12:7)."[9] Because the charisms are ministries to the Church and to the world, they are not to be conceived of as optional ornaments. "These charismatic gifts, whether they be the most outstanding or the more simple and widely diffused, are to be received with thanksgiving and consolation, for they are exceedingly suitable and useful for the needs of the Church."[10] Since the Council, a whole new literature has sprung up which speaks of the charismatic structure of the Church, of charisms as the interior principle of order in the Church.[11] Though not expanded in great detail in the conciliar documents, it is contained in a germinal way in article 3 of the first chapter of the *Constitution on the Church*. The text speaks of the Spirit of Christ who, "existing as one and the same being in the head and in the members, vivifies, unifies, and moves the whole body." At this point the Fathers compare the role of the Spirit in the Church to the role of the soul in the human body. The Spirit is the principle of life for the Church as the soul is for the body. The Spirit vivifies, unifies, and moves "in such a way that his work could be compared by the holy Fathers with the function which the soul fulfills in the human body, whose principle of life the soul is."

Earlier in the same article of the *Constitution on the Church*, the Fathers of the Council indicated how the Spirit functioned as the interior structure of the Church. Speaking within the context of the Mystical Body, the Fathers assert that in that body flourishes a "variety of members and functions." In all of that great variety it is the same Spirit who operates in virtue of his power. "There is only one Spirit who, according to his own richness and the needs and the ministries, distributes his different gifts for the welfare of the Church (cf. 1 Cor 12:1–11)." The Holy Spirit, then, is the principle of unity, because this same Spirit lives in the head and in the members, vivifying and unifying the various ministerial functions.

The charismatic renewal recognizes its own theological presuppositions in this teaching of the Council. In no way would it prefer a narrower focus, less trinitarian and less christological. There is, in the renewal, no attempt to form an elitist group which specializes in the Holy Spirit as though the charisms were the property of any group within the Church. Nor do the groups conceive of growth in Christ as a progress from one charismatic experience to another. If the doctrine of Vatican II, with its large trinitarian and christological concerns, is acceptable to those within the renewal, then they cannot conceive of either the ongoing life of the renewal or of what is variously called "baptism in the Holy Spirit," "l'effusion de l'Esprit," "release of the Spirit," "renewal of confirmation," as representing an exaggerated doctrine of the Holy Spirit. The basis of the renewal is trinitarian rather than exclusively the doctrine of the Holy Spirit.

When one speaks of the specificity of the renewal one is not dealing then with a Spirit-cult. If the renewal is in any danger at all, it is in danger of a christomonism, or of a Jesus-cult. There are some facets of the economy of salvation which have fallen from their rightful place in Christian consciousness and the renewal wishes to restore them. The theological reflection which is going on within the renewal does not wish, however, to isolate these facets and give them an exaggerated importance. Rather, the renewal wishes to give the doctrine and experience of the Spirit their due while keeping them in the broad perspective of trinitarian and christological life. In a theological reflection what comes first is not the gifts of the Spirit but the gospel in its totality. The Church, which belongs to that totality, is constituted by two missions: the mission of the Son from the Father, and the mission of the Spirit from the Father and Son. Any renewal within the Church which forgets the broad perspectives of the gospel and the economy of salvation and builds the Good News out of either the mission of only the Son or of only the Spirit will be doomed to a spiritual poverty. It will have a segmented, narrow theological perspective typified by those who have found a luminous fragment and think they have found the whole. Among the best expressions of the charismatic renewal (and that is the agreed basis of judgment), I do not find that systematic narrowness but rather a desire to see everything in its place and to embrace the whole.

THE OBJECTIONS OF YVES CONGAR

Yves Congar has raised some issues which need clarification. Though the quotation is long, it merits citation in full.

The movement which is called Pentecostal is experiencing a remarkable growth in our midst, above all in the form of prayer groups . . . I am able to say immediately that while posing certain questions, I evaluate the movement positively. The purpose of this small article is much more limited, namely, to draw attention to points of vocabulary.

People often speak as a matter of fact of the "charismatic movement," "charismatic prayer," "charismatic Christians." I have before me an announcement of an international "charismatic conference" to be held in California the days before Pentecost, 1976. It is said that the planning committee includes "Roman Catholic charismatics," that a week will be devoted to national "charismatic conferences." It is against this usage that I make my protests, and I do so with some vigor. It concerns the insupportable abuse of the word "charismatic."

This usage, first of all, takes the term back to a restricted meaning from which the Council tried to free it. I refer to the restriction of the meaning to extraordinary phenomenon: speaking in tongues, prophecy, and the gift of healing. Now these things most certainly concern what St. Paul called the charisms, but they are only particular forms of them. St. Paul speaks also of charisms concerning marriage and the vocation of virginity, the gift of consolation, the gift of presiding, and even, finally, of charity. These are the gifts of nature and of grace which the Lord is using for the building up of his body which is the

Church. It is in this way that the Council speaks of them (*Lumen Gentium*, art. 11). One remembers the day when Cardinal Ruffini rose up in the Council and protested against the mention of charisms in the schema on the Church. There had been such things, he said, in the first days of the Church, but those days had passed.

The next day Cardinal Suenens gave a reply to Cardinal Ruffini and did so with excellent biblical documentation. Cardinal Suenens added: "One should not think that the gifts of the Spirit consist exclusively of extraordinary and astonishing phenomena . . . Do not all of us know, each in his own diocese, lay people, men and women, who are truly called by God. By the Spirit they have been given various gifts in matters of catechetics, in evangelization, in all forms of Catholic Action, and in social and charitable apostolates."

This citation introduces the second point of our critique. The usage which we challenge, and of which we have given some examples, tend to reserve the term "charismatic" to certain Christians and to make a specialty of it. Now if one takes the word in the larger sense in which St. Paul used it (which the Council repeated), one is not able to admit this more restricted usage. I do not accept, either for myself, or for the Christian people active in the work of God, to be excluded from among the charismatics. A great number of men and women have gifts of the Spirit which they put in the service of the kingdom.

This concerns the reality on which our bishops touched in their proclamation at Lourdes in November of last year, under the title of *One Church Entirely Ministerial*. This is to say that the Church is entirely and organically responsible for its own proper vitality which is at the service of its mission. Everything which at this time develops in the theology of ministry is bound to this recognition of the charisms as they are extensively present in the people of God.

The title of "charismatic renewal," says Henri Caffarel, places the accent upon the charisms. The greater part of French

Catholics who are involved in this renewal, prefer the terms "spiritual renewal" or still more briefly, "renewal." Renewal, without a doubt, has the fault of being imprecise, but at least it has the merit of not isolating the movement (*courant*) from other renewal movements in the Church today (op. cit., 6). Could we not settle for the name "renewal in the Spirit," which has been suggested by Msgr. Huyghe?

There is no doubt that a great importance has to be attached to the question of vocabulary. The words define and fix what is represented by them. If you want to think straight you must speak with exactness. We are present at the beginning which is most likely promising. We have to find for it a name which does not cause confusion.[12]

This extensive quote from Yves Congar raises some substantive issues which are reflected in the vocabulary current in the renewal. Père Congar objects, quite rightly, to the restriction of the term "charism" to such gifts as speaking in tongues, prophecy and healing. This narrowness of view does find some expression at the popular level. At this level many speak of the gifts of the Spirit and in fact mean only the more attention-getting gifts mentioned in 1 Cor 12:28. Congar's protest is well taken. An impoverishment results if one speaks of the gifts of the Spirit in such a way that only healing and the word gifts (speaking in tongues, interpretation, prophecy, word of wisdom, word of knowledge) are intended. One can find such expressions within the renewal. However, if one looks closely at the more sophisticated literature issuing from the renewal one will see that what the renewal intends is the full life in the Spirit, which means the exercise of all the gifts in the community. Though the renewal does point to the above-mentioned gifts as aspects of life in the Spirit which have been neglected, by no means does the renewal intend to say that these gifts are necessarily higher than other gifts of the Spirit. Nor does the renewal wish to focus on them in any exclusive way. Those who observe the renewal from the outside often interpret the insistence that all of the gifts of the Spirit are real possibilities for the life of the Church today to mean that the focus is exclusively on these word gifts. This is a misreading of the renewal and its objectives.

The author would like, however, to take issue with placing charity as one charism among many. St. Paul never uses the Greek word "charismata" for charity. There is, of course, a very real sense in which charity, along with faith and hope, are in a more radical sense gifts than any of the charismata which are so commonly associated with the charismatic renewal.[13] Though the argument from silence is always hazardous at best, it does seem significant that in the very context where he is treating of charismatic gifts he does not apply the same term, charismata, to charity as he does to prophecy and tongues.[14] The reason is to be found in chapter 13 of 1 Corinthians. Charity, like faith and hope, in a more radical way anchors one in the life of God than do the charisms; they root one in God at a more primary level. In the hymn to charity of chapter 13, Paul is not suggesting that one chose between the charisms on the one hand and charity on the other. He is saying that charity belongs to a more essential, primary order of our life in God and is therefore the matrix of the charisms, the context in which they are to operate. Within the framework of chapter 13 it is obvious that Paul is saying that one chooses both charity and the gifts (cf. 1 Cor 12:7).

However, if persons would be using the word "charism" in the restricted sense of which Congar speaks, namely, of limiting charism to the word gifts, then his objections are well taken. Generally the more theologically competent in the renewal (and one must here include many laymen) would not so limit the term.

Congar is disturbed by what looks like a sequestration of a term by a few, namely charism, thereby denying that every true Christian has a charism, and denying that every Christian is a charismatic. The intent of the renewal is quite the opposite. Those involved are saying that the full spectrum of the gifts of the Spirit belong to the nature of the Church and to day-to-day life of the local parish. They are indeed insisting that the charisms belong to the many rather than to the elite few. Note also that in speaking of the gifts, the primary point of reference is not the individual but the community. Charisms are ministries to the community, services to the body. A definition of the charism in individualistic terms is a perversion of Paul's thought.

In relation to the sequestering of "charism" Congar raises the larger problem of the vocabulary: "charismatic movement," "charismatic prayer," "charismatic Christians," "charismatic conference." This problem is best understood not only against the background of the renewal's understanding of what a charism is and how a charism is related to the whole Church, but also against the background of the terminological shifts which have taken place within the movement in the few years of its existence.

The movement began by calling itself "the Catholic Pentecostal movement." Almost immediately it became apparent that the word "Pentecostal," so rich in biblical content, was a stumbling block for many Catholics. The term identified the movement within the Roman Church with the movement within classical Pentecostalism (namely, the Assemblies of God, the Pentecostal Holiness Church, etc.). The identification was not with classical Pentecostalism as it actually exists in many places, but with the public image of classical Pentecostalism. This public image included such elements as fanaticism, emotionalism, biblical literalism, credulity, panting after miracles. It did not greatly matter that this public no longer reflected the realities of classical Pentecostalism in many parts of the world. This was the image by which the Catholic Pentecostal movement was judged. As soon as the word "Pentecostal" was spoken, this was the image which was evoked in the public consciousness. In order to avoid this confusion, the Catholic movement came to be called "the Catholic charismatic movement."

"Movement" also brought with it overtones which were undesirable. At the popular level many thought that movement connoted an apostolate organized and structured by interested and committed individuals. This seemed to place the emphasis not on what God was doing among his people, but what man was doing for God. A deep conviction was to be found among those involved that what was happening "was a move of God."

The term "movement" is taken from cultural anthropology and it is a conception which is useful in examining the dynamics of growth in patterns of social change. All of the factors present in other movements of social change such as Mau-Mau, Viet Cong, SDS, Black Panthers, Black Power, Civil Rights, are to be found in the charismatic movement. As in other movements there is a segmented cellular organization composed of units which are bound together by various personal, structural, and ideological ties. Growth is usually effected by face-to-face recruitment by persons already committed to the ideology of the movement and are already participants in its activities. The recruitment usually exploits those personal contacts which already exist (a young man may recruit his brother, his cousin, a woman who works in his office, his father or mother). A commitment act of some kind is usually associated with full membership. The commitment act is usually something atypical of the broader behavioral patterns, such as killing a white man for the Mau-Mau, ambushing American soldiers for the Viet Cong, killing a white policeman for the Black Panthers, breaking into the college president's office and smoking his cigars for SDS, and prophesying or speaking in tongues for those in the charismatic renewal. By virtue of the commitment act an individual separates himself from those who follow the established order, the great mass of the uninitiated, and now identifies himself with the new set of goals and values articulated in the ideology. This commitment act not only separates the person from the great mass of the uncommitted but also commits one to change patterns of behavior. Each movement has its ideology which structures goals and values and provides a framework within which events and experiences can be interpreted. Finally, there is a real or perceived opposition from society at large.[15] In the Catholic charismatic renewal all of these factors are present. Therefore the term "movement" is appropriately applied to it.

One of the objections to the term "movement" is based on the supposition that in a movement there is one head to whom all are responsible. Further, it is supposed that in some monolithic fashion there are prescribed patterns of organizational life so that small chance for organizational creativity or spontaneity exists. When the term "movement" is used by cultural anthropologists the contrary is more often asserted. Movements are many-headed, polycephalous. Who is the head of the Black Power movement, to whom all within the movement are answerable, recognized by all as the one head? None exists. Or what is the universally accepted pattern of group life and activity within the Black Power movement? None exists. So also in the charismatic movement. There is no one person who stands at the head of the movement. It is polycephalous. Nor is there any one prescribed structural form for community life, acknowledged as valid for all and binding on all. The movement is pluriform in its life.

At the more popular level the term "movement" is transferred from cultural anthropology and placed in a theological context. Now a kind of distortion takes place. Some suppose that the charismatic renewal, because it is a movement, sequesters the Holy Spirit and the gifts. If one wants to receive the Holy Spirit or find where the gifts of the Spirit are exercised, then one goes to the movement which has this special concern. With some frequency those who use "movement" in this sense restrict the meaning of charism to the word gifts: tongue, prophecy, interpretation, word of wisdom, word of knowledge. Because of the possibility of misunderstanding, "Catholic charismatic movement" was set aside by large numbers of adherents, and the phrase "Catholic charismatic renewal" was adopted.

This phrase has come under criticism, especially in Europe, and not only by Père Congar. From what has already been said, it is evident that the renewal does not represent a sequestering of the charisms. Those within the renewal do not claim that they alone have the Spirit or the charisms. They are saying that the charisms belong to the whole Christian community, if only it will allow itself to be opened up to the full spectrum of what the Spirit has to offer.

Several years ago at a lecture on the charismatic renewal in Southern France Max Thurian asked if all renewals were not charismatic. The answer to this must be Yes. The implication is that no one movement should appropriate to itself what is common to all renewal movements.

Those within the charismatic renewal in the United States assert that the charismatic renewal no more lays special claim to the

Spirit and the charisms than the liturgical movement lays special claims or appropriates the sacraments and the Church's liturgy. Both movements point to aspects of the mystery of salvation, confronting the Church with questions, asking whether or not this or that aspect of that economy of salvation has been lived to the full. No appropriation has taken place in the charismatic renewal.

In order to avoid the suspicion that the movement has appropriated as its exclusive heritage what is the common treasure of the Church, the author, when lecturing in Europe, referred to the movement simply as "the renewal." There was an outcry in the question and answer period. With some indignation one person in the audience suggested that it was presumption of a rather high order to call this movement the renewal. As a matter of fact, there are a number of renewal movements in the Church. There are also a number of "spiritual renewals" in the Church. Seemingly the phrase "renewal in the Spirit" is open to all the objections made of the other phrases applied to the movement.

However, Père Congar is fully justified in his objection to such phrases as a "charismatic Christian," "a charismatic priest," or "charismatic prayer." These phrases unnecessarily isolate those in the renewal from other Christians.

Père Congar adverts to the statement which the French episcopate issued in November 1973, entitled "A Church Completely Ministerial." This document was not accessible to me, but I take it from the title, and from the context in which Congar quotes it, that the French bishops are speaking about the ministerial structure of the Church, namely, every Christian has, by reason of being a Christian, a ministry to the Church and world.

At this point those in the renewal and the French bishops are of one mind. First, both would want to insist on the ministerial structure of the Church, that is to say, the charismatic structure of the Church. A charism is defined in terms of ministry. Charisms are manifestations ($\phi\alpha\nu\acute{\epsilon}\rho\omega\sigma\iota\varsigma$) of the Spirit (1 Cor 12:7), a coming to visibility of the Spirit who operates ($\grave{\epsilon}\nu\epsilon\rho\gamma\epsilon\widehat{\iota}$) in each for the common good (1 Cor 12:6), that is in the service of the

Church and the world. The body of Christ is indeed constituted of members who minister to each other (1 Cor 12:26). The unity and order of the whole comes from their common principle, the Holy Spirit who manifests himself in a variety of ministries for the common good. For Paul, it is supposed that each Christian has a ministry which is directed toward the common good. The ministry of each is determined by that particular charism each is given. A radical egalitarianism, in virtue of which each Christian can do everything and anything, is excluded by the charismatic structures of the Church.[16] Each can exercise only that ministry for which he has received a charism. The ministerial structure of the Church is such that the one Spirit manifests himself in a variety of charisms. There are varieties of services to be rendered, but only one Lord (who is Jesus); there is one power in action in all kinds of different ways, but it is the same God (the Father) acting in all of them (1 Cor 12:4–6). One Spirit, one Christ, one Father, but a variety of different ministries.

The inner structure of the Church is itself ministerial, directed outward to service rather than inward toward self-perfection. This harmonic ensemble of unity and variety has as its goal the "common good" (1 Cor 12:7), the "building up" of the Church (1 Cor 14:3–25). This structure of mutual ministries is variously called "the body" (1 Cor 12:12–27), "one body in Christ" (Rom 2:5), and the "body of Christ" (1 Cor 12:27; Eph 4:12). Because Paul takes his point of departure from the "body of Christ," a living organism of mutually supporting members, Paul has this perception of an ensemble of charisms which are ministries, of which the Spirit is the active principle. The Spirit gives them unity and an ordered life. In its interior structure the Church is ministerial.

The charismatic renewal has looked upon "helpers and administrators" (1 Cor 12:28) as well as "prophets, teachers, workers of miracles, those with gifts of healing" (1 Cor 12:27–28), and those with many languages (1 Cor 12:27–28), to be part of that ministerial structure. These charisms are not seen as private privileges, not as unusual graces or extraordinary gifts, but ministries which belong to the normal life of the local church, building up that body through a mutuality and complementarity of services. Because all the charisms are ministries, altogether they are comparable to that harmony of purpose, that mutuality of servanthood, that simplicity of unity which is found in the harmonious ensemble of the human organism, the body of man (1 Cor 12:12–30). As in a human body, so in the charisms there is a mutual penetration in their convergence.[17] The one Spirit working in this astonishing variety of ministries makes "the one body" (1 Cor 12:12).

The charismatic renewal does not have as its purpose to isolate any one gift or gifts from this harmonious whole, and attribute to it (or them) an exaggerated importance. Rather, it is saying that if that harmony is to be maintained then all of the charisms should find a place in the daily life of the Church, each in its proper function and with its own proper dignity.

Here, too, the charismatic renewal would point out that there is no suggestion in the biblical text that all the gifts are of equal merit or dignity. Quite the contrary, Paul indicates a hierarchy of dignity (1 Cor 12:28). Those gifts which more immediately and in a more substantial way minister to the community are higher than those which less immediately and in less substantial ways minister to the whole body. A ministerial order based on the charisms is not an order where everyone, in virtue of that person's charism, is equal to everyone else. The prophet exceeds the worker of miracles because his ministry is more immediate to that day-to-day life of the community. Neither the worker of miracles nor the speaker in many languages shares the degree of immediacy to the life of the local church that the prophet does.

Père Congar speaks of "the gifts of nature and grace which the Lord is using for the building up of his body . . ." This raises the problem of the nature of the charisms. Here two extremes need to be avoided. Some have an exaggerated supernatural view of all the charisms. For these the charisms appear to be entirely new capacities, new faculties which were not present before the Spirit came to visibility in the new form of ministry. In this view the emphasis is on the action of the Spirit endowing the community with capacities which are beyond those of any other community of persons. At a given moment the Spirit begins to act in a new mode of action which has about it the character of an intervention from beyond history. God breaks through time and through the laws of creation to effect a new work. Those who belong to this school of thought see the charisms as of a completely different order of things from natural capacities. Some would go so far as to see all charisms as essentially miraculous manifestations.

At the other end there are those who see the charisms as expressions of psychological states or simply the redirection of a natural capacity toward a religious end. Charisms are identified with one's inherent capacities. They have sociological functions.

Between these two views one finds those who see the charisms as a new dimension in the power of the Spirit of life of the local church (or the Church Universal). This newness is not to be found in giving a radical new capacity nor in serving a new sociological function, but rather in the Spirit energizing with his power those capacities which belong to a full humanity. The Spirit makes his own the potentialities of man, energizes, vitalizes them with new powers, and directs them toward the building up of the body of Christ.[18]

In this view speaking in tongues and prophesying would not radically differ from what takes place in certain pagan cults. What makes them different in a Christian community is their mode. They are exercised in the power of the Spirit and have a new finality, that is the kingdom of God. This view in no way diminishes the charisms. But it does guard against the danger of over-supernaturalizing them, making each exercise of them a miraculous intervention on the part of the Spirit. But they wish to acknowledge that the Spirit is free and sovereign and he works when, how, and where he wills. Finally, the Spirit operates with the demonstration of power: "My speech and my message were not in plausible words of wisdom but in demonstration of the Spirit and of power" (1 Cor 2:4). This moderate view of the charisms in no way denies the possibility of a miraculous intervention from within history by the Spirit.

THE IMPARTING OF THE SPIRIT AND
THE CELEBRATION OF INITIATION

The relation of the religious experience, variously called "baptism in the Holy Spirit," "l'effusion de l'Esprit," "release of the Spirit," has been explained in two international statements.[19] Here only the briefest summary will be given.

By all indications Paul considered water baptism the locus of the giving and receiving of the Spirit (1 Cor 12:13; Eph 1:13). Paul knew of no post-baptismal rite which conferred the Spirit.[20] For Paul it was unimaginable that one could be a Christian apart from the impartation of the Holy Spirit. To be a Christian was to have received the Spirit for it was precisely the function of the Spirit to join one to Christ. "If a man does not possess the Spirit of Christ he does not belong to him" (Rom 8:9). In Paul the supreme moment for the imparting of the Spirit is baptism.[21] "Baptism, in its New Testament context, is always a baptism of the Spirit."[22] In the earliest Pauline writings the actuality of the Spirit, no matter how imparted, ruled the apostle's thinking. His attention is more on the Spirit than on the immersion in water by which the Spirit was bestowed. Like Christ, the Christian is anointed by the Spirit, and this sharing in the anointing is a sign that the believer has entered with Christ into the Messianic age where the Spirit will be poured out on all flesh.[23] Gradually the images that the apostle used to speak about the imparting (anointing of the Spirit, sealing, receiving the Spirit, earnest of the Spirit [2 Cor 1:21]), became fixed language for speaking about baptism and its effects, and finally became technical terms for the sacraments through which the Spirit is imparted. "The actuality and fullness of the Spirit of God, whose 'outpouring' is most closely connected with baptism, dominates the apostle's field of vision."[24]

Though Luke distinguishes between water-bath and the reception of the Spirit, he places them in relation to one another. There is abundant evidence that the reception of the Spirit was associated with baptism (Acts 2:38; 10:44; 19:1–7). In Luke the full rite of Christian initiation comprises hearing the gospel, repentance in accepting the word of God, reception of the Spirit, and entrance into both the Church and the new age of eschatological fulfillment, though the temporal sequence in Luke varies.[25] It should be acknowledged that Luke presents a certain ambiguity since he both distinguishes between water-bath and the coming of the Spirit, and establishes a pattern of relating the two. One could emphasize the distinction (to the point of separating the two), or one can focus on the relatedness. Whatever the exegetical decision, Luke wanted the Pentecost event related in Acts 2:1–13, 37–41 to be the model of Christian baptism. This initial outpouring of the Spirit belongs "to the antecedents of Christian baptism."[26] As an antecedent it would seem to identify baptism as the locus of the reception of the Spirit.

Whereas the mention of baptism in most other New Testament texts is direct and clear, those found in the Johannine writings are indirect and in the nature of allusions. This has given rise to controversy on the presence or absence of sacramentalism in the Fourth Gospel.[27] The position taken here is that John represents a moderate interest in the sacraments, while rejecting the temptation to interpret John's Gospel as a secret but aggressive sacramentalist. Here only two texts will be examined.

John 1:25–34. The superiority of Christ's baptism over that of John is emphasized. The superiority is expressed in words placed in the mouth of John the Baptist. This suggests that John's baptism will cease now that Christ has introduced the baptism in the Holy Spirit. Very likely the phrase "to baptize with (or in) the Holy Spirit" refers both to the nature of Jesus' messianic mission and to the baptism of the new covenant, which gives the Spirit. It would seem that the weight of meaning would be on the nature of the messianic mission which is to bring the Spirit, rather than narrowly on water baptism as such.[28]

John is given first a vision of Jesus as the one whom God has designated and filled with the Holy Spirit (cf. 3:34; 7:37–39).

This Jesus who has had the Spirit come down on him "and remain," has been filled with the Spirit, is the Messiah, he who baptizes in the Holy Spirit. The actual water baptism through which the Spirit is given is the symbol of the inner nature of Jesus' mission. He gives the Spirit. Oscar Cullman notes that at the beginning of John's Gospel there is reference to Christian baptism by the Lamb who has removed the sin of the world and has therefore fulfilled the meaning of all baptism and brought baptism in the Spirit.[29] John alone of the evangelists stresses that the Spirit "remained" in Jesus. In the Fourth Gospel it was not a question of a momentary manifestation of the Spirit, but that the Spirit took possession of Jesus who now baptizes in the Spirit.

John 3:5. "I tell you most solemnly, unless a man is born through water and the Spirit, he cannot enter the kingdom of God." Given the integrity of the text,[30] the meaning of the text seems clear: entrance into the kingdom of God is by means of a rebirth in baptism which is both a water-bath and a bestowal of the Spirit. In the Johannine context, "spirit" means "reality," or "absolute being." This reality is living, powerful, and life-giving.[31] It refers to a supernatural birth which is called rebirth.[32] John is concerned about the fundamental process of salvation which, for the early Church was linked with the sacrament of baptism. Though Jesus' words to Nicodemus include the water-bath in which the Spirit is given, the main preoccupation of the evangelist is not "directly with baptism, but with the new creation by the Spirit of God."[33] The "new thing" in Christian baptism is the bestowal of the Spirit.[34] That this new thing is mentioned so casually and without any extended explanation appears strange to us. Even while enjoying the fellowship of the Holy Spirit, and in the very act of appealing to the manifest work of the Spirit among them as evidence that the messianic age had begun, those who belonged to the first days of the Church did not reflect in any marked degree upon the Holy Spirit. Nor in the first days of the Church did they elaborate any doctrine about the fellowship in the Spirit or his manifestations. Paul was the first to do so in his epistles.[35] However, what is clear from the New Testament evidence is that the bestowal of the Spirit belongs to Christian initiation, to the making of a Christian.

No attempt will be made to trace the early history of how this biblical teaching on baptism became part of the initiation practices of the early Church. Only a few aspects of this history will be touched on.

The post-apostolic Church took over the New Testament teaching on baptism and, in the light of Paul's teaching that baptism is a dying and rising with Christ, placed the rite of baptism in an Easter setting. Easter was the celebration of the central mystery of the faith and thus was properly the context for the making of a Christian. Integral to the Easter mystery was the feast of Pentecost. It was the Risen Christ who sent the Spirit and therefore Pentecost was an Easter event. Already about the year 200 Tertullian witnesses to the Easter-Pentecost mystery as the baptismal mystery.

The celebration of the Eucharist as part of initiation is not found in the New Testament but is attested to by Hippolytus (c. 217) who claimed that his teaching in general represented what was already an ancient tradition. To become a Christian was to become a member of a Christian community. Therefore, the candidate who had been immersed and had hands laid on him was led into the Christian community already assembled where they together celebrated the Eucharist.

Initiation was entrance into the central Christian mystery, Christ's triumphant passing over from death to life. This mystery was rich, indeed complex, with the totality of the gospel. In the mystery was included redemption, the centrality of trinitarian life, the moral demands of the gospel, the focus on Christ, the coming of the Spirit, and the eschatological fulfillment. Initiation meant entry into all of this. How does one express this richness and complexity in a way which is understandable?

The early Church took as its point of departure the one Easter mystery celebrated by one initiation. They thought of it as one mystery and one initiation even when the rites were many and were spread over a period which included the somewhat extensive catechumenate. In examining how the Church celebrated the

Easter mystery, one does not start with the multiple ritual acts and thus arrive at a unifying theme. One starts with the integrity of the one Paschal mystery and with the integrity of the ritual expression of that mystery. To express ritually the richness of the Easter event, the early Church developed a cluster of rites: the instruction of the catechumens, exorcisms, anointings, handing over of the creed, blessing of the water used for immersion, water-bath, laying on of hands (or anointing), clothing with a white garment, and celebration of the Eucharist. Though this one, integral initiation varied in its constituent elements from place to place, and from one period of history to another, it was considered to have its own integrity as one initiation. There were occasions when one or the other element was separated from the whole rite (postbaptismal anointing postponed a considerable length of time after the water-bath). Frequently enough this was done for reasons which were neither pastoral nor theological in motivation. Still the celebration of initiation retained its essential integrity well into the early Middle Ages[36]; one Easter event celebrated by one initiation.

The integrity of initiation has been labored here because it is essential when speaking of how the post-apostolic Church related the coming of the Spirit to initiation. In this history the coming of the Spirit was related now to one element (water-bath), now to another (laying on of hands or anointing). Since the early Church was articulating the richness of the one Paschal mystery (which includes Pentecost) in one initiation celebration, it distorts the meaning of the baptismal celebration if one ritual element (water-bath or laying on of hands) is examined in isolation from the whole celebration. Though the early Church rightly attached specific meaning to specific ritual acts, they were not universally consistent in what meaning or function they attached to these acts. This makes it imperative that the whole be kept in mind in interpreting how the early Church conceived the making of a Christian. If this is not done we read back later historical developments into the early period. This is especially true for what later became confirmation, which represents a splitting off from the sacrament of baptism and erection into a separate, distinct sacrament.³⁷ When reading patristic texts which speak of an imparting of the Spirit by the laying on of hands distinct from the water-bath, one should remember that the Fathers were generally thinking of one initiation celebration, not of isolated ritual acts. We tend not to think of the integrity of initiation and therefore attribute a meaning to the patristic texts which would be alien to the Fathers who wrote them.

Not infrequently among the prayers to be used in the celebration of initiation was a prayer that the candidate receive the Holy Spirit. In the *Apostolic Tradition* of Hippolytus, chapter 22 (which comes from about 215), there is a prayer said by the bishop. After the candidates have come up from the water-bath and while the bishop is laying his hand on them he prays that they will "be filled with the Holy Spirit."³⁸ In his treatise "On Baptism," chapter 8, Tertullian speaks of a laying on of hands and uses the forceful image of an hydraulic organ, with which water and the hands of the performer are used to produce melody. In the same way, Tertullian says, the water of baptism and the hands of the minister call forth the Holy Spirit.³⁹ But in Tertullian the emphasis is on the laying on of hands as the rite for imparting the Spirit.

In two Syriac documents, *The Teaching of the Apostles* and *The Acts of Judas Thomas*, there is no laying on of hands or anointing after the water-bath as found in Tertullian,⁴⁰ Hippolytus, and Cyprian. This seems to represent a common Syriac tradition. One would not want to say that because these specific rites are not found in the Syriac celebration of initiation, the Spirit was not given.

Cyril of Jerusalem (c. 315–386) attributed the imparting of the Spirit both to the water-bath and to the anointing which followed the water-bath. Cyril said that the water-bath "conveys to us the gift of the Holy Spirit."⁴¹ But he also says that the anointing "causes in us the Holy Spirit."⁴²

These few historical references are sufficient to see that the imparting of the Spirit belongs to the nature of Christian initiation, seen as a whole, even though this imparting of the Spirit was expressed ritually in different ways. The various ways in which the Church gave ritual expression should make us wary of attaching the imparting of the Spirit to any one element of the initiation celebration, for instance, attaching it exclusively to the post-baptismal anointing which was later to be split off from the initiation celebration and become an independent rite of confirmation. Finally, well up into the early Middle Ages there was no other imparting of the Spirit which constituted the ordinary Christian in the fullness of the Spirit than those rites which belong by their nature to Christian initiation. The totality of the rite by which one made a Christian was what we now recognize as baptism, confirmation, and Eucharist, each of which had its constituent parts which varied from place to place and from one period to another.

That one is not talking about relics of the past which have no real relation to life today, it should be noted that the new rite of baptism for adults wishes to restore the unity of the rite of initiation. Baptism is not to be given to adults without confirmation and the celebration of the Eucharist. The text of the new rite reads: "According to the ancient practice maintained in the Roman liturgy, an adult is not to be baptized unless he receives confirmation immediately afterward, provided no serious obstacle exists. This connection signifies the unity of the paschal mystery, the close relationship between the mission of the Son and the pouring out of the Holy Spirit, and the joint celebration of the sacraments by which the Son and the Spirit come with the Father upon those who are baptized."[43] The reason given for the celebration of baptism and confirmation within the one liturgical event is that it "signifies the unity of the paschal mystery," a point which has been stressed in this exposition.

Though there is no real evidence that the kind of charismatic manifestations which accompanied the baptismal practices recounted in Luke, already described, namely, prophetic utterance and praying in tongues, were to be found in close proximity to the celebration of initiation, they were present in the local churches and were considered a normal part of the life of the Church. Ignatius of Antioch speaks in generic terms of the church at Smyrna as being "endowed with all the gifts of the Spirit, lacking no spiritual grace."[44] In what might be a eucharistic context the author of the Didache says, "Prophets, however, should be free to give thanks as they please," and there are detailed instructions for handling situations where prophets are active.[45] At this early date bishops and deacons are taking over the work of the prophets. In the *Apostolic Tradition* Hippolytus, who has been laying down regulations on the use of laying on of hands, speaks about those who have the gift of healing. "If any one among the laity appears to have received a gift of healing by a revelation, hands shall not be laid upon him, because the matter is manifest."[46] Irenaeus speaks of heretics who "do not acknowledge the gifts of the Spirit and cast from themselves the prophetic grace by which man is watered and by which he bears fruit in life to God."[47] Shortly afterward he speaks of those who "do not receive the Holy Spirit, that is, they despise prophecies."[48] To reject the gift of prophecy was to reject the Holy Spirit and a sign of heresy.[49]

One can, of course, dredge up references to charismatic prophetic experiences from the silt of this early history, but it must be recognized that in quantitative terms the evidence after Montanism is not impressive. There are several reasons for this. First, the early post-apostolic Church, like the Church of the New Testament itself, did not reflect theologically on the experience of the Spirit and the fellowship the early Christians shared in him. There is not a single treatise dealing specifically with the person of the Spirit composed before the second half of the fourth century. The Council of Nicaea (325) was brief to a fault. All it had to say on the subject of the Holy Spirit was "And (we believe) in the Holy Spirit." Secondly, the Church seems to have overreacted to Montanism, a charismatic, enthusiastic revival movement which rose in Phrygia in the second half of the second century. There were very likely many excesses which called for censure, but the reaction of the Church from this time on was such that whenever a charismatic manifestation appeared among the people she remembered Montanism and she identified prophecy with the excesses of this early movement. Thirdly, when the Church did turn her attention to the person of the Holy Spirit it was not to his experienced presence, but to his nature; more precisely, was he a divine person in the sense that the Father and the Son were. There was a great deal of confusion on this subject, to the point where St. Gregory of Nazianzus could write that "to be only slightly in error (about the Holy Spirit) was to be orthodox."[50] Fourthly, there is an inherent obscurity in the Holy Spirit, who is Breath, not to be found in the Son, who is Word. There is a further concreteness to the Son who became Man and lived a human life among us, not to be found in Spirit who was experienced as present but who did not take human form and does not have that human history.

That the Spirit was imparted and received in baptism was one of the arguments in these early centuries for proving that the Spirit was divine in the same sense as the Father and the Son. The argument proceeded in this way: In baptism one receives the Holy Spirit and is "deified," made like to God. In the celebration of baptism one is initiated into the Godhead because one receives the Holy Spirit.[51] If one rejects this one rejects salvation itself. So went the argument.

If these early Christians were asked to locate "the baptism in the Holy Spirit," they would point to the celebration of initiation (baptism, confirmation, Eucharist) by virtue of which the Spirit is imparted and received in his fullness. What the contemporary charismatic renewal calls "baptism in the Holy Spirit" belongs to the making of a Christian and does not belong to a later, more mature stage of the Christian life.

SPECIFICITY OF THE CHARISMATIC RENEWAL

In the light of this history the question must be asked, What is the specific focus of the charismatic renewal? It is best to start with an even more specific question, If the theological locus of "the baptism in the Holy Spirit" is initiation, and all who have been initiated have received it, what do those in the renewal mean when they speak of a "baptism in the Holy Spirit?"

"Baptism in the Holy Spirit" is used in the renewal in two senses. First, there is the theological sense. Anyone who has been initiated has received the baptism in the Holy Spirit in this theological sense. Secondly, there is an experiential sense. When at the popular level persons ask, "Have you received the baptism in the Holy Spirit?" it is to this experiential sense that they refer. The question points to an experience, either of a given moment or unfolding over a long period of time, when what was received at initiation emerges or breaks into concrete consciousness. This need not be seen as a new imparting of the Spirit but rather the Spirit already present becomes a fact of conscious experience. Experience in this sense need not be accompanied by any emotional elevation but, as any experience, does not exclude the emotions. Those who have had this experience most frequently speak in categories of presence. There is a perception at the experiential level of the person of Jesus in his Lordship as real with a new immediacy. This reality does not come from beyond, nor from an abstract sense of pervasive, all-embracing presence. Rather, this reality emerges from the kind of "hereness" which only a concrete person can have. A reality which is not vision but is direct, immediate, concrete, the opening from now and here to the interior of another's consciousness. Above all this reality is experienced as personal and concrete. The person thus experienced is Jesus.

There is also a perception at the level of conscious experience of the Spirit. Those who have had the experience speak in categories of power. The power is directed first of all to the presence of Jesus. It is by the power of the Spirit that Jesus is real, concrete, personal. Beyond this power is experience as a new source, not one's own but accessible to one, for the works of mission. Though there is a contemplative quality to the concrete experience of Jesus as Lord, a resting in his presence, there is a further quality of moving beyond this personal moment to mission. Power is experienced as a personal force, an urgency not accountable in terms of one's own history, to proclaim the Lordship of Jesus to the glory of the Father. It is this experience of the presence of Jesus by the power of the Spirit which gives the renewal its special character. Because this experience is seen as a release at the conscious level of what was already received at initiation the charismatic renewal is essentially trinitarian and sacramental and more specifically represents a renewal of baptismal realities and consciousness.

Though this breaking into conscious experience plays a role of some importance, the renewal does not subsume the whole of the gospel under experience. Life in Christ is not seen as a movement from experience to experience. Such a conception would surely be a perversion of the gospel. Within the renewal, as in all authentic expressions of the gospel, persons walk in faith and darkness and in pain as well as in light and joy.

In the theological sense of baptism in the Holy Spirit those in the renewal do not differ from others who have been initiated. All receive the Holy Spirit. All receive some gift of the Spirit. They do differ to the degree that there is a pattern of experience at the conscious level of the Spirit and his gifts which is not discernible, *as pattern*, outside of the renewal. How does one account for this pattern of experience? To some extent the pattern is influenced by the subjective dispositions of those in the renewal. Though subjective dispositions do not determine religious experience, they do affect it.

The Spirit comes to visibility and is manifested in his charisms which are service functions. Imagine that the gifts of the Spirit were represented by a spectrum whch extends from A to Z. Actually the gifts of the Spirit are without number and therefore one cannot limit them by saying they extend from A to Z. But for pedagogical purposes one supposes that the gifts of the Spirit extend from A to Z. In the section of the spectrum which extends from A to P are all those gifts of the Spirit which claim so little attention: almsgiving, service to the poor, caring for the sick, teaching history, doing housework. Any service to others done under the power of the Spirit for the establishment of Christ's kingdom is a charism. In the section of the spectrum which extends from P to Z are those charisms which are more attention-getting, namely prophecy, tongues, interpretation and healing.

The pattern of experience in the renewal differs from that outside in that those in the renewal are saying an adult "yes" to their initiation with expanded awareness, openness, and expectancy. They are aware that the whole spectrum, from A to Z and not just from A to P, are ministries which belong to the normal life of the Church. Because they belong to the normal life of the Church they are not to be considered unusual graces or extraordinary events.

The charismatic renewal is not suggesting that all the charisms in the P–Z section are superior to the charisms in the A–P section of the spectrum. Nor is the renewal only concentrating on the P–Z section of the spectrum. Rather, it is saying that the Church should be open to the full spectrum of how the Spirit comes to visibility. Because those in the renewal have an expanded awareness, expectancy and openness with regard to this spectrum, the pattern of experience within the renewal tends to be different than among those who have more restrictive awareness and openness. The specificity of the renewal is to be found partly in its more expanded openness.

One must briefly mention a caution. Though the Spirit ordinarily deals with us where we are, he is in no sense bound to do so. He blows where, when, and how he wills. And he is in no radical sense dependent on the subjective dispositions of individuals or communities.

Note that one is saying "yes" with expanded expectations to what one received at initiation, that is, to the Spirit. The renewal is not suggesting that it is giving to the Church something she did not already possess. Quite the contrary. The renewal is suggesting that the local churches (and the Church Universal) open themselves up to what they already possess. Cardinal Suenens uses the image of the organ. It has three keyboards, foot pedals, and forty stops (or forty different ranks of sound types). These all represent the gifts of the Spirit. If the local church is using only one of the three keyboards and only four of the forty stops, then in musical terms, the Church has limited itself. The renewal is saying: The organ is already in the possession of the Church. The Church should use all three keyboards, the foot pedals, and on occasion, various combinations of the forty stops. This whole range of possibilities is already accessible to her, indeed, belongs to her as a free gift of the Spirit.

In summary the charismatic renewal points to the experiential dimensions of the Christian life though it recognizes that all is not experience. Charisms are ministries, service to others, and they belong to the normal, everyday life of the Church. There is a larger range or spectrum of gifts than most Christians are aware of and therefore the renewal suggests that communities expand their awareness, openness and expectancy so that the Spirit can come to visibility along the full spectrum of ministries to the Church and the world.

FOOTNOTES

1 *Pentecostalism: a Theological Viewpoint* (Paulist Press, New York, 1971), p. 211.

2 *Constitution on the Church*, art. 2.

3 Ibid., 3.

4 Art. 4.

5 Ibid.

6 Ibid.

7 Ibid., 12.

8 Ibid.

9 Ibid.

10 Ibid.

11 Karl Rahner, *The Dynamic Element in the Church* (*Quaestiones Disputatae*, 12) (Herder and Herder, New York, 1964); Hans Küng, *The Church* (Sheed and Ward, New York, 1967); Gotthold Hasenhüttl, *Charisma, Ordnungsprinzip der Kirche* (Herder, Freiburg, 1969).

12 Yves Congar, "Charismatiques, ou quoi?" *La Croix*, 19 Janvier 1974. Though some of these objections may remain, Yves Congar acted as a theological consultant to an international group of theologians and pastoral leaders which, together with Cardinal Suenens, issued "Theological and Pastoral Orientations on the Catholic Charismatic Renewal." Father Congar indicated that some of the theological objections raised in the above-quoted article had been answered in this document and he signed it as a consultant. Cf. footnote 19.

13 It is possible that one is given a special gift of faith, over and above that gift mentioned in 1 Cor 13:13. This would be the unusually intense gift of faith which moves mountains. Cf. 1 Cor 12:9; 13:2. One could also have a special ministry, that is, a charism of charity and hope. It would seem that faith, hope, and charity would be used in a different sense from that used in 1 Cor 13:13.

14 I take exception to the exegesis of Heinz Schürmann who considers charity as one of the charisms. "Les charismes spirituels," *L'Église de Vatican II*, ed. Guilherme Barauna, du Cerf, Paris, 1966, vol. 2, p. 553. In 1 Cor 12:31 Paul does not identify the higher gifts with charity. Rather, Paul is telling the Corinthians that of the gifts they should esteem such gifts as prophecy higher than they do the gift of tongues. As is clear from chapter 13 Paul is not saying that charity is a greater charism, but that it belongs to a more fundamental, essential order of spiritual reality.

15 Luther P. Gerlach and Virginia H. Hine, *People, Power, Change: Movements of Social Transformation* (Bobbs-Merrill, Indianapolis, 1970). The basic argument of this book appeared in Gerlach and Hine, "Five Factors Crucial to the Growth and Spread of a Modern Religious Movement," *Journal for the Scientific Study of Religion*, vol. 7 (Spring 1968), pp. 23–40.

16 Ernst Käsemann, *Essays on New Testament Themes* (*Studies in Biblical Theology*, no. 41) (SCM Press, London, 1964), p. 76.

17 Schürmann, loc. cit., p. 552.

18 Cf. George T. Montague, "Baptism in the Spirit and Speaking in Tongues: A Biblical Appraisal," *Theology Digest*, vol. 21 (Winter 1973), pp. 342–60. This material was reworked and published as *The Spirit and His Gifts* (Paulist Press, New York, 1974).

19 "Statement of the Theological Basis of the Catholic Charismatic Renewal," *Worship*, vol. 47 (November 1973), pp. 610–20. It also appeared in *Review for Religious*, vol. 33 (March 1974), pp. 344–52. In leaflet form it is available from Dove Publications, Pecos, New Mexico 87552. This statement was drawn up at the suggestion of Cardinal Suenens for an international meeting of leaders in the Catholic charismatic renewal in Grottaferrata, October 1973. A more extensive statement entitled "Theological and Pastoral Orientations on the Catholic Charismatic Renewal" (sometimes referred to as the Malines Statement) was also the result of Cardinal Suenens initiative. The document was signed by an international team of theologians and pastoral leaders who gathered in Malines, Belgium, May 21–26, 1974. In preparing the final draft, Kilian McDonnell had the written suggestions of theological consultants not personally involved in the renewal: Avery Dulles, Yves Congar, Michael Hurley, Walter Kasper, and Joseph Ratzinger. This document is available from *Word of Life* Publishers, Box 331, Ann Arbor, Michigan 48107.

[20] Ignace, De la Potterie, and Stanislaus, Lyonnet, *The Christian Lives by the Spirit* (Alba House, Staten Island, N.Y., 1971), p. 85.

[21] G. R. Beasley-Murray, *Baptism in the New Testament* (Macmillan, London, 1963), p. 275.

[22] H. W. Robinson, *Baptist Principles* (Kingsgate Press, London, 1938[3]), p. 77.

[23] Rudolf Schnackenburg, *Baptism in the Thought of St. Paul* (Herder and Herder, New York, 1964), pp. 90, 91.

[24] Ibid., p. 91. Oscar Cullman, *Baptism in the New Testament* (SCM Press, London, 1950), p. 41.

[25] R. E. O. White, *The Biblical Doctrine of Initiation* (Eerdmans, Grand Rapids, Mich., 1960), pp. 199, 200.

[26] Edmund Schlink, *The Doctrine of Baptism* (Concordia Publishing House, St. Louis, 1972), p. 26.

[27] For the question of sacramentalism in John cf. Raymond E. Brown, *The Gospel According to John*, I–XII (Doubleday, Garden City, N.Y., 1966), CXI–CXIV. A fuller exposition by Brown is found in "The Johannine Sacramentary Reconsidered," *Theological Studies*, vol. 23, 1962, pp. 183–206. Cf. also White, op. cit., pp. 247–64; Beasley-Murray, op. cit., pp. 216–42. Rudolf Bultmann, *The Gospel of John: A Commentary* (Basil Blackwell, Oxford, 1971), p. 138, footnote 3 et passim.

[28] J. Guillet, on the contrary, refers the phrase "to be baptized with the Holy Spirit" entirely to the mission of Jesus. Cf. "Baptism and the Spirit," *Baptism in the New Testament* (Helicon, Baltimore, 1964), p. 93.

[29] *Early Christian Worship* (SCM Press, London, 1953), p. 65.

[30] Bultmann, op. cit., p. 138, footnote 3, considers the mention of water in this verse to be "at least very doubtful" and is in his opinion the "insertion of the ecclesiastical redaction." Not only other Protestant exegetes have accepted this view but an increasing number of Catholics, among them Braun, Léon-Dufour, Van den Bussche, Feuillet, Leal, De la Potterie. Among those who do not consider "water" to be an addition are Raymond Brown, Cullmann, Dodd, Barrett, Gilmore.

[31] C. H. Dodd, *The Interpretation of the Fourth Gospel* (Cambridge University Press, Cambridge, 1963), p. 226.

[32] Schnackenburg, *The Gospel According to St. John* (Herder and Herder, New York, 1968), vol. 1, p. 369.

[33] Ibid., pp. 369, 370.

34 White, op. cit., p. 254. Cf. also C. K. Barrett, *The Holy Spirit and the Gospel Tradition* (SPCK, London, 1947), p. 124.

35 Dodd, *The Apostolic Preaching and Its Developments* (Harper, New York, 1962), p. 59.

36 J. D. Davies, "The Disintegration of the Christian Initiation Rite," *Theology*, vol. 50 (1947), pp. 407–12.

37 Roger Beraudy, "Recherches théologiques autour du rituel baptismal des adultes," *Maison Dieu*, no. 110 (1972), p. 39.

38 To be found in E. C. Whitaker, *Documents of the Baptismal Liturgy* (SPCK, London, 1960), p. 6.

39 *Corpus Christianorum: Series Latina:* 1:283.

40 *Didascalia Apostolorum*, ed. R. Hugh Connolly (Clarendon Press, Oxford, 1929), pp. 146, 147. "The Acts of Judas Thomas" in *Documents of the Baptismal Liturgy*, E. C. Whitaker, ed. (SPCK, London, 1960), pp. 10–16.

41 *Mystagogical Catechesis*, 3:3; *Sources Chrétiennes*, Cyrille de Jérusalem, *Catéchèses Mystagogiques* (du Cerf, Paris, 1966), p. 124.

42 *Mystagogical Catechesis*, 2:6; *Sources Chrétiennes*, p. 114.

43 *Ordo Initiationis Christianae Adultorum*, no. 34 (Typis Polyglottis Vaticanis, Vatican City, 1972). Aidan Kavanagh interprets this rite to mean that the initiation of adults is regarded as the normal practice. Cf. "Christian Initiation of Adults: The Rites," *Worship*, vol. 48 (1974), p. 334.

44 *To the Smyrnaeans, Greetings; The Apostolic Fathers*, ed. K. Lake (*Loeb Classical Library*) (Harvard University Press, Cambridge, 1945), vol. 1, p. 250.

45 *The Didache*, 11, 12, 13; ibid., pp. 324, 326.

46 *The Apostolic Tradition*, p. 15; *The Apostolic Tradition of St. Hippolytus*, ed. Gregory Dix (SPCK, London, 1937), p. 22.

47 *The Proof of the Apostolic Preaching*, p. 99; *Patrologia Orientalis*, eds. R. Graffin and F. Nau (Firmin-Didot et Cie, Paris, 1919), vol. 12, p. 730.

48 *The Proof of the Apostolic Preaching*, p. 100; ibid., p. 731.

49 For other charismatic manifestations cf. Hans von Campenhausen, "Prophets and Teachers in the Second Century," *Ecclesiastical Authority and Spiritual Power in the Church of the First Three Centuries* (Stanford University Press, Stanford, 1969), pp. 179–212.

50 *Orations*, 21:33; PG 35:1121.

51 Amphilochius of Iconium, Synodal Letter (PG 39:96–97).

Baptism in the Holy Spirit:
Pastoral Implications

RALPH MARTIN

So much of what we have called "renewal" since Vatican Council II has occurred mainly on the theological or conceptual level. We see it much more in books, articles, and documents than in the lives of the Christian people. That is why the charismatic renewal, and what is happening in it on the grass roots level, is so important. It is especially significant for those who are responsible for making the connection between the "renewal on paper" and the renewal that must take place in the hearts and lives of the people of God. I believe that the experience of the reality described in the charismatic renewal as "baptism in the Spirit" as it is experienced even now on an increasingly international scale has many pastoral implications for us. It will be the purpose of this paper to explore some of these implications.

First of all, in terms of its fruits, what is "baptism in the Spirit?" It is an experience with God that produces in the subject a new or greater desire for prayer; a substantial increase in his hunger for and understanding of scripture; a greater awareness of the presence of God; an increase of love and the ability to express that love. These changes are often accompanied by at least some degree of improvement in patterns of sin, as well as a lessening of emotional difficulties so that the person is able to live in a more free and loving way as a Christian. Frequently also, the experience is accompanied by one or another of the charismatic gifts of the Spirit, listed, although not exclusively, in 1 Corinthians 12. The most commonly experienced of these is the gift of speaking in tongues for private prayer.

When one turns to the meaning of the baptism in the Spirit at this more pastoral level, one relates it to what theologians are writing about it. One of the great weaknesses of contemporary theology has been its lack of contact with the pastoral facts of life. An example is the way much of Catholic Missiology speculates on what must happen for the world to believe. These conjectures are often removed not only from clear and relevant scriptural principles, but from the full range of contemporary pastoral facts of life. Once I heard a Catholic Chilean missionary learnedly explain to an audience that people of the Third World would never accept the gospel without first having their social lot transformed. Once again the now popular untruth was being enshrined that "people can't accept the gospel if they're hungry; we need to change their environment before we can preach the gospel." I found his talk particularly disconcerting because I had recently talked at length to those who knew that Chilean Pentecostals were having great success in bringing men and women in the barrios of Chile to a fervent, committed Christian life. Then, as a consequence of their personal conversion, a social and economic transformation was taking place. The same is true in Brazil and other places where the personal stability and social solidarity brought by the Pentecostal experience has resulted in remarkable social and economic improvement in the lives of the "oppressed."

When we make theological statements about the pastoral and dogmatic implications of baptism in the Spirit we run the same risk; we too can be in danger of speculating without sufficient contact with the extensive experience of real persons. We must keep closely in touch with baptism in the Spirit as people are experiencing it. We need to assemble and examine the necessary data. We need to recognize that theology in part flows from an experience of God, and is an attempt to explain that experience and make it coherent. The theological reflection of the New Testament and the early Church was based on their encounter with Jesus and his Father, and their remarkable, continued experience with the Spirit Jesus sent to them at Pentecost.

For this chapter I would like to submit personal accounts by three very committed Catholics who describe what they experienced before and after baptism in the Spirit.[1] I would like then to use these reports of actual experience as one of the bases for establishing some pastoral implications of baptism in the Spirit for the Church as a whole. What is presented here is obviously not gathered and classified by a scientific statistical method. Nevertheless, I believe it is quite representative of the experience people in the mainstream of committed Catholicism have had with baptism in the Spirit. Because it is representative I believe it is worth serious consideration.

An eighty-four-year-old nun:

For over sixty years of my religious life, I could not meditate. I tried every method; the sisters tried to teach me, but all in vain. The best I could do was to read little prayers and try to keep my mind on what I read. After receiving the baptism of the Holy Spirit, I am living a new life. Christ has become real. He is alive. I feel his presence in me, around me. When I read Holy Scripture it means something to me. Now I can see meaning in the Bible stories; they apply to me; they are real. Christ talks to me; I talk to him. Meditation is a real spiritual joy. Time goes so fast; an hour slips by before I'm finished talking with him. Even my love for people is different . . . The peace and joy I now experience cannot be described. After all these years, at the age of eighty-four, I am beginning a new life. I have a new awareness of Christ's presence in my life. Praise the Lord.

A rector of a seminary:

I felt personally inadequate before a job for the first time in my life. Many times I had tried to be number one, doing everything by myself, only to have things end in ruin. When I was studying at Harvard, I tried so hard to be the best student that they finally had to carry me off to the infirmary for some rest. Later I became a Judge Advocate in the Air Force and immediately tried to solve all the military justice problems in the Eastern United States. Again I collapsed from exhaustion. I did the same thing in some of my inner city work, letting the problems and the work load build up to the point of collapse. This time I knew I couldn't wait until the work ended in disaster before turning to the Lord for help. I told the Lord that this was the end, and did my best to ask him to take over.

I hadn't read anything about Catholic Pentecostals except some sensational headlines and stories about kooky things going on at Notre Dame and I was not inclined to pursue it. Yet when a very close friend of mine, the superior of a women's Carmelite monastery nearby, told me about being baptized in the Spirit, I don't remember even questioning what she said. We sat in the visiting room of the seminary and she just told me very simply what had happened to her since being prayed with. I thought to myself, "Yes, yes, this has to be for me. If being baptized in the Spirit can make such fantastic changes in her after years of living the contemplative life, then it's definitely something I need right now."

I had to wait about five weeks. I read a little, but mostly just got more and more hungry for the Spirit. Then, Fr. Jim Ferry from New Jersey came to the seminary with a group of young people to give a talk. His talk was about Christ and every time he mentioned the name "Jesus" it was like someone setting off sparks in me. The desire for Jesus was so strong I felt it would break through my chest. Later, Fr. Jim asked if anyone wanted to pray for anything. Before I knew it, I was kneeling in the middle of a group of about thirty people asking to be baptized in the Holy Spirit. They laid hands on me and immediately I received a tremendous peace right down to the balls of my feet. It completely filled me with a new sense of being, deep within me. It was glorious. I later joined a group praying over a priest for an increase in wisdom. But every time I tried to pray over this man in English, it came out in another tongue. That night, I woke up about twelve times to find myself praying. It was prayer I had never known before, a beautiful sense of the Holy Spirit crying out inside me.

My life and work as a priest changed totally and dramatically. My preaching became a proclamation of the Good News of

Christ. My counseling started to include more prayer for healing. My confessional work started to involve revelatory gifts such as knowing what a person's problem was before he said it, or seeing a completely different approach to a problem than the one the person had. Prayer itself eventually took on a more contemplative orientation. I violated the rules I set for myself as a busy college administrator and gave the time between eight and ten every morning to the Lord, and found that I accomplished more between ten and twelve than I used to between eight and twelve.

One of the biggest changes I experienced was a new courage and strength to state what I knew was right, even though my statements might be uncomfortable and unpopular. This happened most dramatically in connection with the conspiracy trial of Fr. Philip Berrigan and the others in Harrisburg.

A *Catholic bishop*:

For me a bishop is someone who has to unite a local church. As I began to experience the pluralism, indeed division, in the Church today, I started looking for an answer, some way to make the Church one. I noticed how St. Paul handled the problem of polarization between the Hellenists and the Jews in the early Church. He didn't approach it directly but rather drew their attention to the person of Jesus, insisting that in Jesus we find the key to the answers we are seeking to all our problems. I knew that what I was looking for as a key to the unity of the Church had to do somehow with centering our lives on Christ.

I went to a theological institute on Jesus Christ and listened to theologians. I came back feeling sad because I didn't find the answer, only questions. But then in the experience of a prayer retreat, led by a priest who was deeply involved in the charismatic renewal, Fr. George Kosicki, I found the key. It is centered in the realization that Jesus Christ is Lord. Our whole theology can be plugged into that statement, and it pulled things together for me. I think we're taking the heart of Christianity—the person of Jesus—for granted. When we're attracted to that person, in personal union with Him, then He will teach us the truths that keep us in unity. He will communicate His vision of reality. Sometimes even in statements that we bishops put out we're a little heavy on "the Church teaches." Sometimes we don't quite make clear that centrality of commitment to the person of Jesus that is needed to make the teachings make sense and to motivate people.

At the end of that retreat I asked to be prayed over for a deeper work of God's Spirit in me. That began my contact with the charismatic renewal, and the deepening of my own prayer life and experience of the working of the Spirit. This power of the Holy Spirit that has been released in my life through the charismatic renewal became particularly clear to me when I had to give a retreat for priests. As you know, giving a retreat for priests these days is quite a challenge. I think I spent two months preparing for it and had eighteen talks ready. But then I felt I should go away for a day just to pray and fast to prepare for it. During that day the Spirit began to show me that, in addition to preparing talks, I had to be open too and to expect His help and guidance on the spot. The Spirit said that I had to be open to Him helping me understand where the men were and what their real needs were. And the experience of that retreat was tremendous for me because I found priests listening.

At the end of the retreat an older priest came up quietly just to say, "Bishop, I'm deeply grateful for this retreat. I don't recall in fifty years ever having attended one that had this kind of power with me. We really needed this." My reaction was one of "Isn't this wonderful! Praise the Lord!" but at the same time, I wondered if the young priests had been reached. Then three young priests came to me after the retreat to say they felt they were beginning to find their way out of confusion. They attributed this feeling primarily to the insistence during the retreat that we must center our lives on Jesus Christ and be men of prayer.

I had a similar experience giving a retreat at a seminary where the seminarians were terribly divided and the community fragmented. On the retreat I preached the basic gospel message, of the living person of Jesus as Lord. Afterwards the rector said that the results of the retreat could be summed up in the remarks of one student who put it like this: "Before the retreat I didn't think that even Jesus Christ could unite this community, but somehow He did it through the bishop."

These are results of a power working through us that we can't claim originates with us; it is the power of the Holy Spirit Himself, and it produces results far beyond what merely human effort alone produces. It is this working of the Spirit through me, in preaching, in counseling, in prayer, that I've begun to experience in a new way through the charismatic renewal.

One can't lean too heavily on a limited sample, but there are things worth noting about the experiences of these three Catholics. First, they are all living committed lives as Catholic Christians and have had all the formation benefits that the Church currently provides. All of them speak of a substantial inadequacy in their basic experience as Christians *and* in their ability to fill their function in the work of the Church in a way that bears fruit. The nun had a serious difficulty in her basic experience of Christ and in her ability to pray. She also had difficulty living out her vocation as a member of a religious community whose basic commitment was to love one another. The seminary rector had a significant difficulty in "keeping it together" and in being effective in his work as a priest. The bishop had been unclear about the center of Christian life, the person of Jesus, and was unable to function effectively in his role as bishop. Through baptism in the Spirit all experienced significant personal help in their basic relationship with God: they came into a substantially more personal relationship with Christ, their prayer life became more contemplative, they grew in hunger for and understanding of scripture, they experienced deep-rooted personal joy, peace, and other qualities of Christian personality. They also experienced substantial improvements in their ability to function in their particular roles: in loving the brethren, in receiving guidance from the Lord, in having the Holy Spirit a more active partner in sacramental ministry, in more powerful preaching, as well as in other areas.

In the last ten years I have been involved full time in Christian service as a layman: in campus ministry, in work for the national office of the Cursillo Movement, in numerous retreats for priests, nuns, and lay people, in conversations with people from every level of Church life, and from many countries, and increasingly so now in my work in the international charismatic renewal. Relying on this wide range of exposure to Catholicism, I am convinced that the experience of these three Catholics before they were baptized in the Spirit is, if anything, better than that of most committed Catholics in the Church today. Under the term "committed Catholics" I do not include the vast majority of Catholicism's 670 million people who have had nothing like the formation, education, catechesis, and encouragement that the small minority of committed Catholics have had.

I'd like now to talk about why the three Catholics above have experienced baptism in the Spirit in the context of the charismatic renewal and did not do so in the course of their sacramental initiation and subsequent formation. For the purposes of this paper let us assume that the effects of baptism in the Holy Spirit are considered normative for Christian life and initiation, as the majority of professionally involved theologians and scripture scholars maintain.

In no sense do I wish to oppose the religious experience I am now discussing to sacramental life. On the contrary, if the sacraments of initiation were prepared for and followed by the right kind of nurture, this experience would have its full sacramental dimension. I believe that people are having a profound religious experience in the charismatic renewal and not, in most cases, in the immediate context of the sacraments of initiation and their subsequent nurture in the Church. I believe this for the following reasons:

1. In the charismatic renewal there is a clear understanding of and focus on the very core of the gospel message: the reality of sin, the need for forgiveness, the need to turn to Jesus as our personal Lord and Savior, and the gift of the Spirit. In the Church

at large today there is often a confusion about what is at the center of Christianity and a great vagueness about the person of Jesus as seen in the testimony of the bishops. The kerygma isn't very often clearly perceived, understood, and proclaimed with power. Much of the Church is in need of basic evangelism.

2. In the charismatic renewal there is a full biblical awareness of the whole range of the workings of the Spirit, whereas in the Church as a whole there is a diminished awareness of the scriptural witness to the work of the Spirit. For example, in recent years when Catholic education addressed the question of the gifts of the Spirit it spoke only of the gifts of the Spirit mentioned in Isaiah, and nothing of the gifts of the Spirit mentioned in the New Testament, notably the 1 Corinthians 12 gifts, commonly called charismatic. The confirmation catechesis spoke solely of the Old Testament gifts. Teaching about the Holy Spirit in the Church at large has most frequently been neglected or, when taken up has been only partially presented. In the charismatic renewal there is a fuller biblical awareness of the whole continuum of the Spirit's action and manifestations. This fuller awareness allows a person to open up to that fuller range of the Spirit's activity.

3. In the charismatic renewal there is a markedly greater expectancy than in the Church as a whole. The renewal expects that the gifts of the Spirit mentioned in the scripture are intended for the Church of today, indeed are available to every Christian community. These gifts are not something reserved just for the early years of Christianity, or for the canonized saints. Sound biblical exegesis supports the legitimacy of such an expectancy. In many ways the charismatic renewal is the biblical renewal being appropriated by the "man in the pew."

4. Because people in the charismatic renewal are more aware of the biblical promises of God's action among men and because their faith is more expectant, they consequently experience more of the working of the Spirit than does the Church as a whole. The average person in the Church today doesn't know what God has to offer in the way of a vital relationship with Christ in the power of the Holy Spirit. He does not expect to have such a re-

lationship. Consequently he rarely experiences much of a relationship with Christ or the working of the Holy Spirit in his life.

5. The forms of prayer groups and charismatic communities are also important in the scheme of things. They provide environments of Christians who themselves are aware of God's promises in scripture, are expectant in faith, and are experiencing God's workings in their own lives. It is in such environments that most people come into the awareness and expectancy that leads to the experience of baptism in the Spirit. These environments serve not only to introduce people to a fuller Christian life, but to nurture them in it as well. Almost everyone who perseveres in this new life in the Spirit does so in connection with some supportive prayer group or community where this biblical awareness, expectancy and experience is fostered and supported.[2] This support, for a fervent Christian life, and evangelistic power, is seldom found in most of our parish activities and liturgical celebrations.

I'd like now to give a brief sketch of how, practically, people are drawn to a renewal of Christian initiation in an established charismatic community, and then draw some implications for the pastoral task of the Church as a whole.

First, people who have already experienced a renewed life in Christ through the Holy Spirit gather together to express that life together and strengthen it in a weekly prayer meeting; there the Spirit is free to operate in the whole range of his gifts. People who are finding new life in Christ tell their friends and acquaintances and invite them to "come and see" by coming to the prayer meeting. At some point these friends and acquaintances either move toward wanting the same life themselves or decide it's not for them, at least not right now.

When a person expresses interest in establishing or deepening his life with Christ and being baptized in the Holy Spirit, most prayer groups provide an opportunity for him to attend a seven-week instructional series entitled "Life in the Spirit Seminars." The seminars were originally developed by our community here in Ann Arbor as a way of introducing people to a deeper life in Christ and to baptism in the Spirit. They are now used for this purpose by thousands of groups all over the world.[3] The series consists of a simple, direct presentation of the basic truths of the Christian message: the reality of God and of sin, the promise of new life in Christ and the gift of the Spirit. The presentations call people to have faith, and to repent by concretely turning away from sin and toward Christ; they show people how to ask Christ for his Spirit to be released in their life, or to be given for the first time if the person is not already a Christian. Discussion leaders develop a personal relationship with people going through the seminars and talk with them personally outside the seminars about how they are responding to its message. In the fifth week, those that the team leader and discussion leader feel are making an adequate and sincere response to the messages are invited to express their personal commitment to Christ and their renunciation of sin, and to be prayed with for baptism in the Spirit with the laying on of hands. The last two weeks are devoted to basic instruction in growing in the Spirit. That includes an explanation of the importance of vital Christian fellowship and an invitation to continue on with the group.

When the people who put on the seminars have some degree of maturity in the Christian life and are experienced in helping people into such a life, the seminars are remarkably effective. In our own community for example, almost all of the people we pray with in the fifth week have a real experience of the presence of God and the work of the Spirit in their life; the few that do not are able to grow into it over a period of time as they remain in contact with an adequate support group. Over a thousand have been through the seminars in our own city (population 100,000). The testimonies of the three Catholics quoted above can be multiplied a thousandfold by people from a variety of Christian backgrounds and also by those who had not been Christians. A significant grass roots renewal is taking place and it is growing at a remarkable rate.

What are some pastoral implications for the Church as a whole? First, it is apparent that the vast majority of those baptized as infants (almost one million alone in the United States last year) do not, as they grow up, personally appropriate the gift of the Spirit given to them in baptism. I believe this raises serious questions, not about infant baptism, which I heartily believe in, but about our policy as regards its administration.

Those who uphold infant baptism argue that it makes sense because of parents' and godparents' faith as they represent the community of faith, that is, the local parish and the Church Universal. I think this rationale makes good sense, but is seldom observed. Is it realistic to believe that the baby we baptize will ever appropriate the gift of the Spirit given in the sacrament? If the parents and godparents have never appropriated in a personal way the gift of the Spirit, and in some cases do not even believe in the Lord, is it reasonable to expect the baby to? If the local parish is composed mainly of people Catholic in name and Sunday observance only, is it reasonable to administer infant baptism any longer except in specifically adequate situations? Do we not need to develop criteria for when it makes sense to administer infant baptism? We have heard of some parishes in South America which refuse to administer infant baptism except when the parents are practicing their faith. Even this move is but the feeblest beginning in facing the faith condition of the Christian people and the legitimacy of administering infant baptism in that situation. Knowing where to "draw the line" is certainly difficult, but the line is almost nonexistent in most of the Church today.

Secondly, the preparation of adult "converts" is being done in equally questionable ways. There were only 73,925 adult converts baptized in the Catholic Church in the United States in 1973. A relatively small number of these were conversions of non-Christians to Christianity. The rest were efforts to make peace in the family by both spouses being of the "same faith," "conversions" from Protestant churches, and the life. In itself, the statistic is a sad commentary on the vitality of Christian life in the Catholic Church, but when one looks into adult convert programs, it becomes tragic. People are being baptized into the Catholic Church as adults with almost no solid criteria and little solid spiritual preparation. They have little expectancy of what baptism will bring, or what their future life in the Church will be. The results correspond to this kind of preparation.

The same lack of clear criteria and adequate spiritual preparation makes the administration of the sacrament of confirmation in the vast majority of cases pastorally ineffective. Very few of the hundreds of thousands of children and adults who are confirmed each year in the Catholic Church are led into or strengthened in a fervent, Spirit-led, Christian life. Confirmation, like baptism, is often administered in a cultural situation where it is simply expected that at a certain age "everyone is confirmed" with almost no regard for where the "everyone" is in terms of basic commitment to the person of Christ and understanding of and eagerness for the release of the Holy Spirit in their life. It is heartbreaking to see "the whole sixth-grade class" being "prepared" for confirmation and then see them "receive" it with scarcely any tangible results in the way of strengthened Christian living. Courage is needed today to look at the pastoral facts of life. When we do so, the immensity of the disorder and ineffectiveness of the sacramental situation can appear overwhelming. But seeing things "as they are" is the necessary first step in getting them to be where they should be.

The sacraments of initiation are the "quality control" points which determine to a large extent the quality of Christian life in the Catholic Church. The life-giving Spirit of Christ flows into the Church through the sacraments. As they are currently administered, the Spirit indeed may be given, as sacramental theology tells us, but with virtually *none* of the effects that God intends them to bring about. They are certainly not producing a Church of vital Christians. When confronted with such pastoral realities our tendency has usually been to "defend" the sacraments and talk of their "ex opere operato" effects, which indeed they have. But such theological overkill has virtually blinded us from seeing that what the Church today most needs is not a defense of the sacraments. Rather, it needs a pastoral offensive that learns how the sacraments are to be administered to truly produce Christians in more than name only, so that they truly become the salt of the earth, the light of the world. It is here, I believe, that the charismatic renewal has many lessons for us.

Reflections like the ones I have been offering are often objected to on the basis of elitism, sometimes with phrases such as "this is a church of sinners, not a sect; remember the parable of the wheat and the tares; only at the judgment were they separated out." I believe this is a fundamental misunderstanding for God's purpose for the Church. The parable does not recommend that the existence of sinners and "saints" in the same Church should determine our initiation policy. Far from it. The gospel clearly states that entrance to the Church of Christ must be by way of repentance, faith in the person of Christ, and the gift of the Spirit, or that entrance is not complete. We see this as a continuing concern of the apostles throughout the first years of the young Church's life as recounted in Acts. The very rigor of the early Church's catechumenate in the early centuries demonstrates how important these steps were for them. Despite our best efforts in preserving the quality of Christian initiation, there will be sin in the Church. But when we are not making those best efforts, we can scarcely claim that we are being faithful to the gospel or adequately proclaiming that gospel to a world desperately in need.

FOOTNOTES

[1] These accounts originally appeared in *New Covenant* magazine; reprinted with permission. An eighty-four-year-old nun: March 1972, p. 5; rector of a seminary: June 1972, pp. 4–5; Catholic bishop: September 1971, p. 10.

[2] Directories of Catholic prayer groups, one for North America and one international, are available through the Communication Center, P. O. Drawer A, Notre Dame, Indiana 46556. Information on other denominational groups is available by writing Episcopal Charismatic Fellowship, 100 Colorado Boulevard, Denver, Colorado 80206; Lutheran Charismatic Renewal Coordinating Committee, c/o The Rev. Larry Christenson, 1450 West Seventh Street, San Pedro, California 90732; Charismatic Communion of Presbyterian Ministers, 428 NW 34th Street, Oklahoma City, Oklahoma 73110. For Baptist charismatic groups, write The Rev. Ken Pagard, First Baptist Church, Fifth Avenue and E Street, Chula Vista, California 92010.

[3] Since the first edition of *The Life in the Spirit Team Manual* was printed in 1971, 65,000 copies have appeared. The manual is for those working on the seminar. Less than a year and a half ago a companion devotional book, *Finding New Life in the Spirit* was published for those taking the seminar. One hundred and ninety thousand copies are in print. *The Life in the Spirit Team Manual* has been translated into Chinese, Korean, German, Japanese, French, Sesouth, Dutch, and Italian.

The Charismatic Renewal as Experience

HERIBERT MÜHLEN

Is a new orientation becoming evident in the Christian churches? From a mood of resignation to a new hope, from uncertainty to a new assurance of faith? Is a spiritual renewal coming from within? Pope Paul VI has said on May 23, 1973, with reference to the Holy Year of 1975 that the emergence of a "truly spiritual (pneumatic), that is, charismatic movement" among the faithful is required. What is meant by this? In the draft "Ministry and Pastoral Service in the Community" prepared for the synod of the German bishops it is stated: "Living communities in which a multiplicity of gifts of the spirit interact and in which all members share a common responsibility for the work of salvation make up one of the most important goals of ecclesiastical renewal."

The crucial question, of course, is how such a renewal of the gifts of the spirit, of the charisms, should be carried out. Can one simply "introduce" something like this as one might introduce liturgical or structural reforms? Or wouldn't it require rather a genuine charismatic break-through throughout the entire Church, a "new Pentecost?" This was the great vision of Pope John XXIII, and Pope Paul VI has frequently alluded to this theme. Is it just coincidental that the first prayer groups in the Catholic Church came into existence (first in the U.S.) a year after the conclusion of the Second Vatican Council (June 1966)? These prayer groups prayed for a renewal of the charismatic gifts, and in them there occurred a break-through to a basic charismatic experience. This idea had already been broached at the Council, admittedly rather cautiously but clearly nonetheless: "The Holy Spirit conferred special gifts on the individual believers and in this way they become fit and ready to undertake the tasks of renewal and of the rebuilding of the Church" (*Constitution on the Church*, art. 12). Who would have imagined that ten years after the publication of this document some 1,500 prayer groups, attended regularly each week by about 200,000 Catholics including some bishops, would exist in the Catholic Church? The first international congress of Catholic prayer group leaders took place in Rome from the ninth to the eleventh of October 1973. One hundred and thirty delegates from thirty-four countries took part, among them Cardinal Suenens of Belgium and two American bishops. On the twenty-fourth to the twenty-sixth of February 1974 there was a meeting in Würzburg of approximately sixty Catholics who make up the steering committee for some twenty-five prayer groups which have emerged in German-speaking countries during the past two years.

In the United States the "Catholic charismatic renewal" is strongly influenced by the mentality and methods of the free Pentecostal churches which arose at the beginning of this century. Such a growth process is completely legitimate, for the Second Vatican Council has expressly stated that the gifts of the Spirit which are alive in the separated churches can contribute profoundly to the upbuilding of the Catholic Church as well. The Catholic Church is by no means reflective of the "fullness of the Catholic spirit" in every aspect of real life (Decree on Ecumenism, art. 4,10). The term "Catholic Pentecostal movement" has not gained acceptance, however, since the Pentecostal churches manifest in some respects a certain one-sidedness and narrowness of outlook which cannot be accepted by the Catholic Church. As a result the term "Catholic charismatic renewal" very quickly became the favored one. Yet the word "charismatic" itself provokes misunderstandings. Very often the image of something extraordinary, of something strange, in short, of a "sect" is evoked by this word. Beyond that, it is clear that not every expression and method of the Americans can be adopted in the country which saw the emergence of the Reformation, pietism, theoretical atheism, and historico-critical exegesis. The term "prayer renewal" would be just as expressive, for the charism of the praise of God for its own sake is the doorway to all other charisms and creates in a person the very capacity to receive the others. This was particularly apparent in the Pentecost experience of speaking in tongues (Acts 2:4–11). Yet, the basic charismatic experience (see below) can and may not ever be sought for its own sake. One must therefore distinguish between the goal and methods of the prayer renewal.

1. The *goal* consists in the first place in seeking to achieve a level of faith which by virtue of a socially transmitted faith experience thoroughly involves and imbues the entire person. The climax of a lengthy process of preparation through instruction, meditation, and prayer is usually a public act of new and radical commitment to Christ on the order of a renewal of baptism and confirmation. The most elementary foundations of faith are being undermined today. And yet the traditional pastoral care of the established churches presupposes faith, a faith into which one has been indoctrinated since birth. Since, however, this faith no longer receives the unambiguous support of a generally accepted Christian culture, the adult Christian at some time in his life must make a personal fundamental decision of surrender to God as a sort of "second conversion."

Such a new level of faith response is not merely the lonely decision of an individual but is always supported by the personal witness of others (cf. Acts 2:37ff.). In the "charismatic renewal" such witness is the task not only of those who hold official positions but is the responsibility as well of each individual Christian. In the New Testament Church every Christian is a "priest" (cf. 1 Cor 2:13; 1 Pt 2:5 etc.). Every Christian, each according to the measure of grace he has received, is a "minister of the manifold grace of God" (1 Pt 4:10). In this sense a second goal would consist of the effort to make each individual Christian fully conscious of the charisms he has received and thus to bring about a renewal of the Church from the inside, including as well a renewal of the ecclesiastical structures.

2. The *method* whereby a believer is led to a personal faith re-

sponse in the New Testament is not some kind of united effort as in a family, nor is it a community experience on the natural order (as for example in the youth movement at the beginning of this century). It does not consist of wordless introspection in a process of self-knowledge (as, for example, in the techniques of oriental meditation). It is rather a direct, personal, public witness of faith. It is for that reason that the so-called "baptism of the Holy Spirit" (cf. Acts 1:8) is conferred with a view to giving witness to others and serving them. The acquisition of a level of praising God which can embrace the entire person including the feelings is never an end in itself, but is the *way* by which God and Christ can involve themselves in the world in the power of their Holy Spirit. If a particular "charismatic" worship service gives the impression that those involved are seeking an experience for its own sake or are on an ego trip or something like that, then it has failed to make this missionary dimension leading from God to man sufficiently apparent. It is only the person who surrenders himself in service to his fellow man who will discover himself in ways new and unconceived. This will come to him as it were as a bonus, for discovery of self is an unmerited gift of God to us.

THE CHARISMATIC-MISSIONARY EXPERIENCE

"Experience" is a direct contact with the presence of God in the community (cf. 1 Cor 14:25) or in life and not one which is *merely* derived from teaching, tradition, and the institution. Getting to know someone through experience involves a direct and immediate association with this person. This produces a particular kind of profound certainty which is irresistible and almost irrefutable. There is a difference in "experiencing" an area by traveling there oneself or simply by reading a travelogue. Everyone must make his own fundamental experiences himself. This holds true for faith experiences too. Yet, in our everyday Christian life we are almost always dealing with traditions, liturgical forms, dogmas and doctrines, institutions and offices, which did indeed *at one time* grow out of a deep experience of faith but which have since become as it were a "congealed" faith. Many things are indeed so conditioned by the times at which they originated that in this current situation of profound change new ways of achieving a direct and living experience with the living God are absolutely necessary. It is quite true, of course, that the Christian faith experience is never absolutely original, for it remains of necessity bound up with the faith and witness of the apostles and with the apostolic experience of the Spirit as it has been proclaimed down through the centuries. This never proceeds in an exclusively vertical direction "from above." In the history of the Church it has its own history and thus also its historical or *social* dimension. Experience of the Spirit is neither completely immediate (as, for example, in an individualistic misinterpretation of the process of justification) nor is it purely horizontal (as in a distortedly socialistic interpretation of Christian community). It never ceases to have something to do with "seeing and hearing," for it is also an experience of the senses and it always takes hold of the *whole* man right down to deepest emotional experiences.

1 Jn 1:1–3 shows this very clearly: "That which was from the beginning, which we have heard, which we have seen with our eyes, which we have looked upon and our hands have handled, of the word of life—that we proclaim to you, for the life was manifested." The eyewitnesses of the life of Jesus through their direct contact with him really *heard and saw* something of the eternal word, of the "Son" and thus also something of the Father, whom we cannot see and hear (Jn 5:37), who dwells in inaccessible light, and whom no one has ever seen or has been able to see (1 Tm 6:16; cf. 1 Jn 4:20). In order to understand the basic charismatic-missionary experience, it is extraordinarily important to remember that God the Father cannot be seen or heard directly. It is equally important to realize that the man Jesus of Nazareth no longer lives among us and that we can no longer see and hear him as such. He has returned to the Father and has given us his Holy Spirit who now "reminds" us of everything that Jesus did and said, of everything, that is, that the contemporaries of Jesus were actually able to hear and to see (Jn 14:26; 16:7–15). But this Spirit of Christ is by no means inac-

cessible. In the Pentecost sermon of St. Peter, Luke records an ancient christology when he has St. Peter say: "Being exalted therefore by the right hand of God and having received of the Father the promise of the Holy Spirit he has poured forth this *which you see and hear*" (Acts 2:33). This sentence refers to the emergence of a form of praise of God which had not been known up to that time (Acts 2:4–11). Whenever we see and hear other men expressing their deep inner devotion to God in praise and prayer, then we see and hear something of the Spirit of God himself, who is acting in them and they in him (cf. Gal 6:4; Rom 8:15). This praise is an action of God himself, who draws the praying Christian into himself. God the Holy Spirit through and with God the Son calls to God the Father.

In a prayer meeting everyone is invited (without in any way being exposed to group pressure) to praise God "in the Spirit" in a very personal, free, and spontaneous way. And because this praise is not carried out silently, in the depths of one's private person but rather is expressed in public, it has as well a social character. This type of very *personal* and at the same time *social* prayer is what is unique in the prayer renewal under discussion here. The personal witness of others to their faith strengthens, intensifies, and stimulates my own faith and hope and love and all those charisms which God has already given to me and to every other Christian. The Spirit of God "appears" (1 Cor 12:7) in them analogous to the way that the Son of God is evident in the man Jesus of Nazareth. The theological implications of the charismatic renewal are trinitarian in a way which is scarcely duplicated in any other traditional aspect of systematic theology.

The Church has always lived in the spirit of its Pentecost-charismatic origin. The religious vows, the world-wide mission of the Church, caritas, indeed, according to Paul, even the administration of community resources—all these are expressions of charisms. On the other hand, the charisms which are operative in the worshiping community (cf. 1 Cor 14:26) have come to be exercised only by the *one* "priest," the president of the assembly. (The historical development which has led to this cannot be discussed here.) As a result, the charismatic renewal has also set for itself the goal of renewing Christian worship. In doing this the intention is to involve the individual in a far greater way than that which has up to now been achieved by the liturgical movement. The break-through into a level of charismatic praise of God is such a profound experience that some people can actually specify the day and hour of their "conversion" to Christ. For others this is a matter of weeks and months. But in any case there is always some profound change in one's life: Many to their great astonishment notice in themselves and others a new delight in reading the Bible, a new joy in praying alone and with others, in celebrating the Eucharist, a new openness to other people, a sensitivity to their problems, the courage to give direct and personal witness to their joy in believeing, a willingness because of a Christian motivation to become involved in the transformation of unjust social and political structures, etc. It is this transformation in one's own life and as a result eventually in the life of the Church which is the important thing and not how many and what kind of charisms a person has.

PRAYER SERVICES

In the first letter to the Corinthians we read: "When you come together, every one of you has a psalm, has a doctrine, has a revelation [of the mystery of God], has a tongue, has an interpretation: let all things be done to edification" (14:26). This is the shortest description of an ancient Christian worship service. The renewal of prayer as described in the two preceding sections has no other purpose than to seek to restore this ancient form of worship. This is not to be understood as an unhistorical escape into an idealized situation of the early Church but rather as a historically conditioned answer to theoretical atheism which rejects belief in the Creator and as a response to the equally portentous atheism of the heart which denies the possibility that the Spirit of God and Christ can be active among men at the present time. Everyone can detect this atheism of the heart within himself through a simple experiment. Let him withdraw a bit to a place where he can be completely alone and try to speak with God aloud and in a very personal way in somewhat this fashion: "My God, I thank you for having made me and for loving me before you created me. I have not called myself into being; neither can I fashion for myself the purpose of my life. I thank you that you have revealed yourself in Jesus Christ and that his spirit in me calls out to you and praises you." When a person hears himself speak in this way with God, perhaps for the first time, he will most likely get stuck after a few sentences. At this point the situation gets critical. One can no longer retreat. At the same time one becomes aware of a certain embarrassment. Why is this?

A prayer service usually begins with the members of the group greeting each other (even in a church). One of the leaders makes some short comments about the service for the benefit of those who happen to be present for the first time. A few hymns are sung accompanied by modern instruments, followed usually by the reading of a passage from the scriptures with a short commentary (clearly no doctrinaire fundamentalism!). Then come a few minutes of *common* silence. This is not a pause where nothing happens (although a beginner often perceives it this way). Rather everyone attempts to let the proclaimed word of God sink deeply and directly into himself, to be attentive to it. Everybody is aware that the same process is going on within everyone else. This is in itself a form of communication which is absent from the typical Sunday Mass. This silence then gives birth to free personal prayers serving as the response to the Word of God. As a concrete example: After the reading of Mk 7:31–37 (the healing of the deaf mute) someone may break this common silence by beginning to pray: "Yes, Lord, we are all deaf, for we are incapable of ourselves of really listening to your word. We are cut off from the true reality of life. We cannot speak, for we are incapable of praising you. We are morbidly turned in on ourselves. Indeed, we don't even have the power of ourselves to turn to you. Others have to lead us to you, and we beg you to give each of us generous guides who will bring us to you. And then speak to each one of us and bid us to be receptive to you. Make us open to your word and free us for the praise of your

Father." Another might then begin to pray: "Lord have mercy, Christ have mercy, Lord have mercy," and everybody repeats this. After the common silence everyone is invited to offer to God praise, thanksgiving, petition as a service to the faith of others, or to start a song, or to report about an event in which the action of God has been experienced. (It is, of course, impossible clearly to distinguish between an experience that proceeds from self and one that comes from grace. So the charism of discernment of spirits can become very important.) Nothing is programmed; nothing is planned ahead of time. Thus, the service has a certain tension and dynamism. But this is far more than mere group dynamics, for the participants are profoundly aware that they are not responsible for establishing the level of encounter, especially not in the Eucharistic celebration which often follows. We do not wish to speak in detail here about the more remarkable charisms, for example, particular forms of praying in tongues and prophecy. It is in any case inappropriate to give undue attention to these, and in German-speaking countries an exaggeration in this matter has in fact not yet been observed.

Of very great importance, on the other hand, is the renewal of confirmation, or in the case of religious, the renewal of vows, and for priests the renewal of ordination. Someone steps forward (at times at the conclusion of a lengthy process during which this decision developed) and utters a personal prayer of new and radical surrender to Christ. He asks those present for their intercessory prayer. A few people, representing the rest of the group and indeed the whole Church, lay their hands on his head and shoulders and recite prayers of petition, thanksgiving, and praise. This is no initiation rite into an elitist community; rather it is an activation of something which was already received in baptism and confirmation with a primary emphasis now on service in and for the Church. From the dogmatic point of view this is a sacramental.

Observers, and that is normally how one begins to participate in these services, often have three main objections. 1. "I can't reveal my personal relationship to God to others." Of course, there is a legitimate area of religious privacy, in the confessional, for example. But nowhere in the New Testament is it said that one's relationship to God is meant to be concealed or that one should repress his religious emotions. The warnings about the "private room" (Mt 6:6) is directed only at those who pray in public in order to put on airs. Ever since the Enlightenment which held that religion is a private matter and has no place "in public" there has been an emphasis in Christian education on the development of a "privateness" which has led to the discrediting of the emotional side of faith. Indeed, this de-emphasis on the emotions had already been largely accomplished by the scholastics who saw faith as an act of reason. 2. A second difficulty stems from prayer that focuses on self and from an emphasis on religious performance. Some will compose words or sentences during the period of silence and then wonder: Is what I want to say good enough and what will the others think of me? And yet the point is not at all to display one's more or less intense piety but rather to serve the others, to edify the congregation. This personal, publicly expressed praise of God assumes at the same time, God willing, the character of proclamation. 3. These prayer utterances strike many at the beginning as being too "naïve." It is, of course, necessary that all the experiences of the "charismatic renewal" be submitted to critical evaluation by the standards of psychology, philosophy, theology, etc. But the other side must be asserted too. We know much too much about God; we adopt a much too adult attitude in his presence, and we have quite forgotten the simple ways of praising him for his own sake.

The following dangers must be pointed out. 1. The tendency toward personal involvement involves the danger of ecclesiastical fragmentation (the free Pentecostal churches are extraordinarily divided) as well as of sectarian isolation (the ideology of the "holy remnant"). It is in this context that the significance of the ecclesiastical ruling office, which in its task of establishing unity takes into account the Church in its entirety and all pastoral possibilities, gains an astonishing new clarity. There has been no confrontation at all with ecclesiastical hierarchy in the Catholic charismatic renewal up to now. On the contrary, the bishops expect spiritual leadership and direction from this movement. Some twelve Catholic bishops are active participants in prayer groups (structural reform!).

2. Another danger is the tendency to replace doctrine with experience and thus to leave the door open to heresy. Most importantly, the relationship between a purely personal experience and an experience proceeding from the Spirit has not yet received sufficient study. Many thoughts, occurrences, and daily events are too casually and uncritically attributed to the word of the Spirit of Christ. Historically speaking this has been the origin of many sects.

The Ecclesiological Context of the Charismatic Renewal

FRANCIS A. SULLIVAN, S.J.

In his first address as Pope to the Fathers of the Second Vatican Council, Paul VI declared "renewal of the Church" to be one of the primary reasons for the convoking of the Council by his predecessor, Pope John XXIII.[1] In its "Decree on the Ministry and Life of Priests," the Council itself put "renewal of the Church" in first place among "three pastoral goals of the Council," which it named as: "inner renewal of the Church, the spread of the gospel throughout the world, and dialogue with the modern world."[2]

WHAT IS RENEWAL OF THE CHURCH?

The Council gives its clearest answer to this question in the "Decree on Ecumenism," where it states: "Every renewal of the Church essentially consists in an increase of fidelity to her own calling."[3] Another text suggests that such renewal will involve "purification" and "penance."[4] But renewal does not mean only the correction of what has gone wrong; it also means positive steps forward, such as those which the Council recognized as already taking place. "Already this renewal is taking place in various spheres of the Church's life: the biblical and liturgical movements, the preaching of the word of God, catechetics, the apostolate of the laity, new forms of religious life and the spirituality of married life, and the Church's social teaching and activity."[5]

The Council's answer to this question is likewise clear and explicit: it is the Holy Spirit who renews the Church. "By the power of the gospel He [the Holy Spirit] makes the Church grow, perpetually renews her, and leads her to perfect union with her Spouse."[6] "The Holy Spirit unceasingly renews and purifies the Church."[7] There can be no doubt that in the mind of the Council, the Holy Spirit is the principal agent of any renewal of the Church. But he requires the cooperation of the men and women who make up the Church; indeed the Church is called upon to renew herself, but she can do this only insofar as she is moved by the Spirit.

> Moving forward through trial and tribulation, the Church is strengthened by the power of God's grace promised to her by the Lord, so that in the weakness of the flesh she may not waver from perfect fidelity, but remain a bride worthy of her Lord: that moved by the Holy Spirit she may never cease to renew herself, until through the cross she arrives at the light which knows no setting.[8]

I think we can best find the answer to this question by examining the principal texts in which the Council has described the role of the Holy Spirit in the life of the Church. While others could also be quoted, the following four passages seem to me to best express the mind of the Council on this subject.

> The Spirit dwells in the Church and in the hearts of the faithful as in a temple. In them he prays and bears witness to

the fact that they are adopted sons. The Spirit guides the Church into the fullness of truth and gives her a unity of fellowship and service. He furnishes and directs her with various gifts, both hierarchical and charismatic, and adorns her with the fruits of his grace. By the power of the gospel he makes the Church grow, perpetually renews her, and leads her to perfect union with her Spouse.[9]

In the building up of Christ's Body there is a flourishing variety of members and functions. There is only one Spirit who, according to his own richness and the needs of the ministries, distributes his different gifts for the welfare of the Church (cf. 1 Cor 12:1–11). Among the gifts stands out the grace given to the apostles. To their authority, the Spirit himself subjected even those who were endowed with charisms. Giving the body unity through himself and through his power and through the internal cohesion of its members, this same Spirit produces and urges love among the believers. Consequently, if one member suffers anything, all the members suffer it too, and if one member is honored, all the members rejoice together.[10]

It is not only though the sacraments and Church ministries that the same Holy Spirit sanctifies and leads the People of God and enriches it with virtues. Allotting his gifts "to everyone according as he will" (1 Cor 12:11), he distributes special graces among the faithful of every rank. By these gifts he makes them fit and ready to undertake various tasks or offices advantageous for the renewal and upbuilding of the Church, according to the words of the Apostle: "The manifestation of the Spirit is given to everyone for profit" (1 Cor 12:7). These charismatic gifts, whether they be the most outstanding or the more simple and widely diffused, are to be received with thanksgiving and consolation, for they are exceedingly suitable and useful for the needs of the Church. Still, extraordinary gifts are not to be rashly sought after, nor are the fruits of apostolic labor to be presumptuously expected from them. In any case, judgment as to their genuineness and proper use belongs to those who preside over the Church, and to whose special competence it belongs, not indeed to extinguish the Spirit, but to test all things and hold fast to that which is good (cf. 1 Thes 5:12,19–21).[11]

It is the Holy Spirit, dwelling in those who believe, pervading and ruling over the entire Church, who brings about that marvelous communion of the faithful and joins them together so intimately in Christ that he is the principle of the Church's unity. By distributing various kinds of spiritual gifts and ministries, he enriches the Church of Jesus Christ with different functions "in order to perfect the saints for a work of ministry, for building up the body of Christ."[12]

A careful reading of the texts just quoted will show that all four stress the role of the Holy Spirit as the giver of the gifts which equip people for various services and ministries in the Church. And one of these texts explicitly links such gifts of the Spirit to the renewal of the Church: "By these gifts he makes them fit and ready to undertake the various tasks or offices advantageous for the renewal and upbuilding of the Church."[13] If it is ultimately the Holy Spirit who renews the Church, and if he does this by "moving the Church to renew herself,"[14] then we can see that one extremely important way in which the Spirit renews the Church is by equipping people with gifts of grace that prepare and dispose them to share in this work of renewal. If such gifts are "exceedingly suitable and useful for the needs of the Church," then they surely have a vital part to play in her renewal. In fact, while the Council did not explicitly use the term, I believe that it did provide the theological foundation for the idea of a "charismatic renewal of the Church." We must now look more closely at the conciliar teaching about the charismatic gifts, in order to get a clearer idea of what such a "charismatic renewal of the Church" would involve.

THE TEACHING OF VATICAN II
ON THE CHARISMS

As on many other issues, the teaching of Vatican II on the charisms marks a break with a commonly held view, but in doing so returns to an authentic tradition solidly based on scripture. In the Council debate, the commonly held view was championed by Cardinal Ruffini, who maintained that while charisms were abundant in the apostolic era, they subsequently became so infrequent as to have practically ceased. In his view, both history and experience contradict the notion that in our day many of the faithful are gifted with charisms, and that such people can be relied on to make a significant contribution to the upbuilding of the Church. On the contrary, he insisted, such gifts today "are extremely rare and altogether exceptional."[15] In Cardinal Ruffini's opinion, it is obvious that charisms have no important role to play in the life of the modern Church.

Six days later, Cardinal Suenens replied, in a speech that has been widely read, since it was published in a volume of Council speeches.[16] For Suenens, the charisms are no "peripheral or accidental phenomenon in the life of the Church"; on the contrary, they are "of vital importance for the building up of the mystical body."[17] While it is true that in the time of St. Paul some charismatic gifts were dramatic and surprising, "we should never think that the gifts of the Spirit are exclusively and principally in these phenomena which are rather extraordinary and uncommon."[18] Nor are the charisms the privilege of a few; rather, "every Christian, educated or simple, has his gift in his daily life . . . Does not each and every one of us here know of laymen and laywomen in his own diocese who are truly called by God? They are endowed by the Spirit with various charisms in the fields of catechetics, evangelization, apostolic action in all its ramifications, in social work and charitable activity . . . Without these charisms, the ecclesiastical ministry would be impoverished and sterile."[19] In conclusion, Cardinal Suenens proposed that the charisms be given a greater emphasis in the Council's treatment of the Church as the People of God.

Cardinal Suenens' view, reflecting a notion of charism which during the decade preceding the Council had been advanced by such eminent theologians as Yves Congar[20] and Karl Rahner,[21] was the one that prevailed at the Council. His proposal that the charisms be given greater emphasis was also ratified, when the

Council approved an emendation suggested by Bishop McEleney of Kingston, Jamaica, for the strengthening and clarification of the conciliar statement about the charismatic gifts.[22] The emended text became what is now the second paragraph of no. 12 of the "Constitution on the Church." I have quoted this text above[23]; let us now look at it more closely, to see how the Council wishes us to understand the nature and function of the charismatic gifts.

The charisms are described as "special graces" by which the Holy Spirit makes people "fit and ready to undertake various tasks or offices advantageous for the renewal and upbuilding of the Church." Such gifts are not the privilege of any class of people in the Church, but are "distributed among the faithful of every rank." The term "faithful" here obviously includes all members of the Church, from the simplest lay person to the Pope.

Some of these gifts may be rare and extraordinary, but others are "simple and widely diffused." But they are all called "special graces." The conciliar text suggests two reasons for this: the *way* these gifts are given and the *purpose* for which they are given. The *way* is special, because it involves a direct intervention of the Holy Spirit in the life of the Church. The Council distinguishes between the way the Holy Spirit works "through the sacraments and Church ministries," and the way he works in distributing his charismatic gifts. The latter is an immediate intervention of the Spirit, in which he exercises his sovereign freedom to allot his gifts as he wills and to whomever he wills, in a way that cannot be foreseen or controlled by man. Such gifts are "special" also by reason of the purpose for which they are given. Unlike the gifts of faith, hope, and love, which are inseparable from the gift of the indwelling Spirit, and which everyone must have in order to be pleasing to God, the charisms are "*distributed among* the faithful"; no one of these gifts is necessarily connected with sanctifying grace. Their purpose, as described by the Council, is to make people "fit and ready to undertake various tasks or offices advantageous for the renewal and upbuilding of the Church." In other words, they are specific gifts of grace which equip people for specific kinds of service. Obviously, love is the basic gift which is the indispensable motive force behind any and every genuine service to others. Without love, as St. Paul reminded the Corinthians, even the apparently most generous and heroic gestures of service would be worthless.[24] So we can say that every genuine charism presupposes the gift of love, which moves the person to employ his gift in loving service to others. But a charism is a "special grace," in the sense that it equips a person in a particular kind of way for a particular kind of service. As the conciliar text says, it makes people both "fit and ready" (*aptos et promptos*)— two words perhaps better translated by the familiar English phrase "willing and able." A charism, then, as understood by Vatican II, can be defined as *a grace-given ability and willingness for any kind of service that contributes to the renewal and upbuilding of the Church.*

Let us now look at some other texts of the Council which can throw further light on the nature and function of charismatic gifts. The following paragraph is taken from the "Decree on the Apostolate of the Laity."

> For the exercise of this apostolate, the Holy Spirit who sanctifies the People of God through the ministry and the sacraments gives to the faithful special gifts as well, "allotting to everyone according as he will" (1 Cor 12:11). Thus may the individual, "according to the gift that each has received, administer it to one another" and become "good stewards of the manifold grace of God" (1 Pt 4:10), and build up thereby the whole body in charity. From the reception of these charisms or gifts, including those which are less dramatic, there arise for each believer the right and duty to use them in the Church and in the world for the good of mankind and for the upbuilding of the Church. In so doing, believers need to enjoy the freedom of the Holy Spirit who "breathes where he wills" (Jn 3:8). At the same time, they must act in communion with their brothers in Christ, especially with their pastors. The latter must make a judgment about the true nature and proper use of these gifts, not in order to extinguish the Spirit, but to test all things and hold fast to what is good (cf. 1 Thes 5:12,19,21).[25]

This text paraphrases much of what had already been said in the Constitution on the Church, no. 12, but there are several new points to be noted. 1. From the reception of these gifts there arises the *right* and *duty* to use them. 2. They are to be used both in the Church, for the upbuilding of the Church, and in the world, for the good of mankind. 3. Those who use them need to enjoy the freedom of the Spirit, but also to act in communion with their brothers in Christ and their pastors. Communion with pastors means respecting their right to make judgments about the nature and use of these gifts; at the same time, pastors are reminded that they are not to extinguish the Spirit.

On two other occasions, the Fathers of the Council addressed themselves explicitly to the question of the attitude which pastors should have with regard to the charisms of lay people.

> Pastors know that they themselves were not meant by Christ to shoulder alone the entire saving mission of the Church toward the world. On the contrary, they understand that it is their noble duty so to shepherd the faithful and recognize their services and charismatic gifts that all according to their proper roles may cooperate in this common undertaking with one heart.[26]

> While testing spirits to see if they be of God, priests should discover with the instinct of faith, acknowledge with joy, and foster with diligence the manifold charisms—whether lowly or exalted—that are given to lay people. Among the other gifts of God which are found in abundance among the faithful, those are worthy of special attention which are drawing many to a deeper spiritual life. Priests should also confidently entrust to the laity duties in the service of the Church, allowing them freedom and room for action. In fact, on suitable occasions, they should invite them to undertake works on their own initiative.[27]

Of course one should not conclude from such texts that lay people are the only ones who receive charismatic gifts. The Spirit "distributes special graces among the faithful of every rank" (*inter omnis ordinis fideles*),[28] where the word *ordo*, while not restricted to the "sacred orders," surely does not exclude them. On one occasion the Council speaks of the charisms of those who preach the word of God: "The ministry of the Word is carried out in many ways, according to the various needs of those who hear and the various charisms of those who preach."[29] The Council also speaks of a missionary vocation as a charism that is found among priests, religious, and lay people:

Every disciple of Christ has the obligation to do his part in spreading the faith. Yet Christ the Lord always calls whomever he chooses from among the number of his disciples, to be with him and to be sent by him to preach to the nations. Therefore, through the Holy Spirit, who distributes his charismatic gifts as he wills for the common good, Christ inspires the missionary vocation in the hearts of individuals. At the same time he raises up institutes in the Church, which take as their own special task that work of evangelization which is the duty of the whole Church. For every person, whether native to the country or foreign, whether priest, religious or lay person, who is endowed with the appropriate natural dispositions, gifts and character, and is ready to undertake missionary work, is marked with a special vocation.[30]

It should be clear by now why the Fathers of the Council would describe such a vocation as a "charismatic gift": it fits perfectly their concept of a charism as a "special grace that makes a person fit and ready to undertake some service for the renewal and upbuilding of the Church." In fact, it is easy to see that every genuine "vocation" to a life of service in the Church—whether to the priestly ministry, to religious life, to missionary activity, or to the lay apostolate in any of its various forms—must be seen as a charismatic gift. At the same time, a person who has received the fundamental charism of such a vocation can also receive more specific charisms, to equip him or her for specific kinds of service. Thus, for example, the Council speaks of various charisms given to those who preach the Word of God.

WHAT WOULD A "CHARISMATIC RENEWAL OF THE CHURCH" INVOLVE?

Now that we have seen what Vatican II meant by "renewal of the Church" and what it meant by "charismatic gifts," it is time to ask what a "charismatic renewal of the Church" would involve, according to the mind of the Council. Even though the Fathers did not use this term, they did provide the elements that go to make it up. I propose that if we simply draw the logical conclusion from the premises which the Council has provided us, we can say that according to the sense of the Council documents, a charismatic renewal of the Church would involve the following elements.

1. It would consist essentially in an increased fidelity of the Church to her own calling. Since the Church, concretely, is the People of God, it would consist in an increased fidelity of each Christian, from lay person to Pope, both to his calling to be a member of the Church, and to his specific calling within the Church.

2. The Holy Spirit would be the principal agent of this increased fidelity, but the Church would also be an active agent; she would be "moved by the Holy Spirit to renew herself." Here again, "Church" means the whole People of God.

3. The Holy Spirit would bring about the renewal by pouring out an abundance of every kind of charismatic gift which the Church needed at that time, on every kind of person who could help in this renewal.

4. The Holy Spirit would move the people to whom he gave such gifts to recognize them, to understand their purpose, and to use them generously in whatever service their gifts equipped them for.

5. The Holy Spirit would guide lay people to employ their gifts in communion with their pastors, and would guide the pastors to "discover with the instinct of faith, acknowledge with joy, and foster with diligence" the charisms of the laity.

6. The Holy Spirit would give to those in authority in the Church the charism of discernment of spirits, so that in making judgments about these gifts they would not extinguish the Spirit, but would test all things by sound criteria and hold fast to what is good.

7. In a charismatically renewed Church, the choice of persons for roles of pastoral leadership (e.g. pastors, bishops, popes) would be made solely on the basis of the demonstrated presence in that person of the gifts of the Spirit that would equip him for such a role. Thus, however and by whomever the choice was made, ultimately it would be the Holy Spirit himself who, by the distribution of his gifts, would designate the leaders for the Church (cf. Acts 20:28—"Keep watch over yourselves and over all the flock of which the Holy Spirit has given you charge, as shepherds of the church of the Lord.").

8. In a charismatically renewed Church, each local eucharistic community would be a body of Christ, in which each member would have his role and his ministry according to the gift which he had received from the Spirit for the upbuilding of the community. In the life of the community, each member would have the opportunity to exercise the gifts which he had received, under the leadership of the pastor.

IS THE CATHOLIC PENTECOSTAL MOVEMENT A CHARISMATIC RENEWAL OF THE CHURCH?

Whatever answer one might give to the question as asked, there can be no doubt as to what the Catholic Penetecostal movement wants to be: it aims at nothing less than the charismatic renewal of the Church. It would be easy to multiply statements to this effect on the part of recognized leaders of this movement; for the present, two can suffice. The first is by George Martin.

The charismatic renewal is a work of the Holy Spirit, giving faith and calling forth faith, creating Christian community and equipping men and women for ministry. *The future of the charismatic renewal within the Catholic Church, then, would appear to be a charismatically renewed Catholic Church.* I believe that the charismatic renewal can be the vehicle whereby the life of the entire Catholic Church will be renewed. I believe that its potential is not merely to be a movement or a sect within the Church—a specialized Department of Spiritual Experiences off in one corner—but to infuse and renew the entire Church. Perhaps a comparison can be made with the liturgical movement. The goal of those engaged in the work of liturgical renewal was not to create a separate movement within the Church and enjoy quality liturgies among themselves; their goal was to renew the liturgical life of the entire Church. In order to accomplish this goal, it was necessary for the liturgical movement to have some organization and identity as a definite movement. Since the enactment of liturgical reforms by Vatican Council II, however, the identity of the liturgical movement as a movement has all but vanished. It is in this sense that the charismatic renewal can be considered a movement—a Catholic Pentecostal movement. The goal is a charismatically renewed Church, not a separate "Pentecostal" organization "for people who go in for that sort of thing." Having some identity as a movement may be necessary for a time in order to accomplish the larger goal. But the larger goal is the significant one: a charismatically renewed Catholic Church.[31]

The second statement which I shall quote is taken from the widely acclaimed address given by Kevin Ranaghan at the Sixth International Conference at Notre Dame in June 1972.

The charismatic renewal in the Catholic Church is the expression or embodiment of a movement on the part of Almighty God for the purpose of charismatically renewing the Church. It is a renewal of the fullness of the gift of the Holy Spirit on every level of Catholic life, especially imparting lively faith in Jesus, a lively sense of worship, and the gifts and ministries of the Holy Spirit. Therefore the charismatic renewal is not an end in itself nor can it have an existence separate from that of the Church. Rather, the charismatic renewal is part of the Church and exists for the renewal of the Church.[32]

Now we must ask what indications there are that God is actually using this movement for the purpose of charismatically renewing the Church. The most tangible fact about this movement is the extraordinary rate at which its "prayer groups" have multiplied, not only in the United States where it began, but also in many other parts of the world, among people of very different cultures.[33] What is most typical of these groups is that they gather at least once a week for a meeting that rarely lasts less than two hours, and actually spend the greater part of this time in prayer. The feature of these prayer meetings that most immediately suggests the presence of a "charismatic renewal" is their resemblance to the Corinthian assemblies described by St. Paul (1 Cor 14:26–33):

> What then, brethren? When you come together, each one has a hymn, a lesson, a revelation, a tongue, or an interpretation. Let all things be done for edification. If any speak in a tongue, let there be only two or at most three, and each in turn; and let one interpret. But if there is no one to interpret, let each of them keep silence in church and speak to himself and to God. Let two or three prophets speak, and let the others weigh what is said. If a revelation is made to another sitting by, let the first be silent. For you can all prophesy one by one, so that all may learn and all be encouraged; and the spirits of prophets are subject to prophets. For God is not a God of confusion but of peace.

In prayer meetings which are taking place nowadays all over the world, ordinary Catholic people, living quite normal lives, do actually pray and sing "in tongues," and speak messages of exhortation, consolation, or admonition, which are accepted by the group as "prophecies." If someone speaks what seems to be a message for the group "in tongues," the group will pray that someone be given the gift of interpretation, and frequently someone does "receive" the sense of the message, in much the same way that a person who "prophesies," "receives" the message which he is to deliver. On occasion the group will pray with evident faith for the spiritual or physical healing of a person who asks for such prayers, and testimonies abound of healings that have taken place.

At this point the question arises: are the remarkable growth of such prayer groups and the phenomena that characterize their meetings, sufficient proof in themselves that we are witnessing a charismatic renewal in the Church? Is someone who insists on looking for further evidence of this, being overcautious or skeptical? I do not think so. After all, St. Paul made it very clear that such phenomena as tongues and prophecy can be had where love is lacking, in which case they are no better than noisy gongs or clanging cymbals (1 Cor 13:1–3). Mathew's Gospel also has a saying of the Lord that probably reflects the experience of the early Church: there can be prophets and wonder-workers whom the Lord has never known, because they are evildoers (Mt 7:22–23). The lesson is clear: the presence of genuine gifts of the Spirit cannot be judged merely from the external phenomena. Rather, as Matthew's Gospel tells us: "You will know them by their fruits" (Mt 7:16).

So we must go beyond the "charismatic phenomena" of these prayer meetings, and ask what deeper indications there are that the Holy Spirit is really at work here. Personally, I find the following factors reassuring.

1) While the "charismatic phenomena" are what is most likely to strike the attention of a newcomer, the attention of the regular members of the group is not centered on them, but rather on the Lord, whom the group has gathered to praise and worship. In my experience, the atmosphere of the meetings is one of genuine prayer, focused on God and the "praise of his glorious grace" (cf. Eph 1:6).

2) The prayer that is characteristic of these groups is not some eccentric "devotion to the Holy Spirit," but is authentically trinitarian: it is prayer in the Spirit, through Jesus, to the Father.

3) In particular, prayer for a new outpouring of the Holy Spirit and his gifts on the group or on individuals, is directed not to the Holy Spirit but to the Lord Jesus, as the one who "exalted at

the right hand of God has received from the Father the promise of the Holy Spirit" (Acts 2:33).

4) Members of these groups are convinced, and work hard to convince all who wish to join them, that such prayer demands a new and total conversion to Jesus, by which a person really accepts him as the Lord of one's life. There is a good amount of evidence that such conversions do take place and bear fruit in people's lives.

5) There is also a healthy emphasis on the need to build Christian communities, where people can find the environment and support they need to grow in the new "life in the Spirit" which they have entered upon. In these prayer communities, people learn to use their gifts not only in worshiping God but also in ministering to one another's needs.

To my way of thinking it is such features of the Catholic Pentecostal movement as these which provide the best reasons for believing that the charismatic phenomena of their prayer meetings are genuine manifestations of the Holy Spirit.

HINDRANCES TO A CHARISMATIC RENEWAL OF THE CHURCH

We must now face the question whether, along with these reassuring features, there are other elements in the Catholic Pentecostal movement which could prevent it from being the charismatic renewal of the Church that it wants to be. Historical examples abound of movements that intended the spiritual renewal of the churches in which they arose, but instead gave rise to sects or new Christian churches. Whether the blame for such a separation in particular cases lies more with the Mother Church or with the group that sought her renewal does not matter here; what does matter is that such a separation, for whatever cause, frustrated the intention of the movement to bring about a renewal of the Church. It would seem that in most such cases, the successive steps that led to a break with the Mother Church can be described as a process of mutual alienation. What people in responsible positions of leadership in the Catholic Church and in the Catholic Pentecostal movement have to be constantly on the watch for, and have to take effective measures against, then, are any features of this movement that could tend to alienate it from the Catholic Church, or alienate the Catholic Church from it.

Others have already treated this question, and I do not intend to try to discuss every aspect of it here.[34] The point I wish to develop is the danger of alienation that can be involved in what some might not think of as a danger area: namely, the use of words. Anyone who thinks that words are unimportant has not reflected enough on the fact that the wrong use of words leads to misunderstanding, and misunderstandings can easily lead to alienation.

To my way of thinking, there are several ways of speaking current in the Catholic charismatic renewal which involve the real danger of alienating the rest of the Catholic Church.

The first is the use of the expression "baptism in the Holy Spirit" to describe the Pentecostal experience. As I have stated elsewhere,[35] my reason for believing that this is unwise is that on scriptural grounds, every Christian who has received the Holy Spirit has the right to think and speak of himself as having been "baptized in the Holy Spirit." The use of this biblical term to describe the Pentecostal experience inevitably includes the corollary that Christians who have not had such an experience have not been baptized in the Spirit. This negation is implicit in the way that Pentecostals use this term, whether they state it explicitly or not. It is equally misleading to use the terms "Spirit-filled" or "living in the Spirit" in such a way as to imply that it is only through the Pentecostal experience that one becomes "Spirit-filled" or enters into "life in the Spirit."

Finally, something must be said about the use of the word "charismatic." It seems that while most people not involved in this movement still tend to use such terms as "Catholic Pentecostals" or "Catholic Pentecostal movement," most people who are involved prefer to use the term "charismatic renewal." The use of this term has led to their speaking of their prayer groups as "charismatic groups," and of themselves as "charismatics."

Unfortunately, this has inevitably led to their distinguishing two categories of people in the Church: the "charismatics" and the "non-charismatics." The former are people who have had the "baptism in the Spirit" and "speak in tongues," while the rest of the People of God fall into the category of the "non-charismatics." So also one hears references to "charismatic liturgies," where the dividing line between "charismatic" and "non-charismatic" seems to be drawn pretty sharply on the question whether one is going to hear anyone "speaking in tongues" or "prophesying" during such a liturgy or not.

Is there anything wrong with such a use of the term "charismatic?" I agree with Yves Congar that there is much that is wrong with it.[36] As in the use of the term "baptism in the Spirit," the problem lies in using the term "charismatic" in such a way that it applies only to the "in-group," and is implicitly or explicitly denied to all others. Until they experience the "release of the Spirit" and "yield to tongues," all other Christians remain in the category of the "non-charismatics." Receiving the "baptism in the Spirit" and "speaking in tongues" is the narrow gate that leads into "charismatic life," and no one can enter except by that gate.

Perhaps no one expresses it in quite those terms—but my point is that the way people in the "charismatic renewal" are using the term "charismatic" can very easily alienate the rest of the People of God who find themselves described as the "non-charismatics." For example, if some members of a religious community belong to a "charismatic prayer group," it is hardly surprising if other religious in the community resent it when they know that they are being referred to as the "non-charismatic" members of the community. The danger of alienation becomes the more acute when a pastor learns that a group of his parishioners who speak of themselves as "charismatics" are rejoicing that they have finally found a "charismatic priest" to lead them in "charismatic liturgy" and offer them "charismatic ministry."

The question at issue here is a basic one for a charismatic renewal of the Church: What is a charism? Who is charismatic? In the first part of this essay I described two conflicting notions of charism that were proposed at the Second Vatican Council by Cardinals Ruffini and Suenens, and I showed that Suenens' view became official Catholic teaching in the documents of the Council. It will be recalled that Cardinal Ruffini wanted to restrict the term "charism" to the unusual phenomena that were frequent in the early Church, but had subsequently become quite rare. Obviously he was thinking of such things as tongues, prophecy, miraculous healings, and the like. Cardinal Suenens—and the Council with him—proposed a much broader notion of charism: as any one of those gifts of grace that equip people for any kind of service useful for the renewal and upbuilding of the Church. Some of these gifts are unusual, but many of them are quite ordinary. Among such gifts of grace that surely must be counted as charisms in the sense of the Council are all genuine vocations to the service of God in the religious life, in the priestly ministry, or in any form of lay apostolate.

Who, then, is a "charismatic?" Is it not clear that anyone who has received any one of these manifold gifts of grace and is using it in the service of God and his neighbor can rightly be called "charismatic?" I am afraid that the current use of the term "charism" and "charismatic" in the "charismatic renewal" reflects the restricted idea of charism defended by Cardinal Ruffini, rather then the broad concept which the Second Vatican Council recognized to be the authentic Pauline idea, and adopted as its own.

Inevitably a narrow concept of charism is going to result in a narrow concept of who and what is charismatic. And this, in turn, results in too narrow a concept of what a charismatic renewal of the Church would involve, and how it can come about. While I believe that God is using the Catholic Pentecostal movement as an instrument for the charismatic renewal of his Church, I am also convinced that it is crucial for the future of this movement that people involved in it realize that as there are other ways of being charismatic than "speaking in tongues" and "prophesying," so there are other ways to a charismatic renewal of the Church than through the narrow gate of Pentecostalism.

FOOTNOTES

[1] Allocution of Pope Paul VI at the opening of the second session of the Second Vatican Council, September 29, 1963, in *Constitutiones Decreta Declarationes* (Vatican City, 1966), p. 911.

[2] "Decree on the Ministry and Life of Priests," n. 12, my translation.

[3] "Decree on Ecumenism," n. 6, English translation in *The Documents of Vatican II*, edited by Walter M. Abbott, S.J., p. 350. (Future references to this translation will be indicated: Abbott.)

[4] "Dogmatic Constitution on the Church," n. 8, Abbott, p. 24.

[5] "Decree on Ecumenism," n. 6, Abbott, p. 351.

[6] "Dogmatic Constitution on the Church," n. 4, Abbott, p. 17.

[7] "Pastoral Constitution on the Church in the Modern World," n. 21, Abbott, p. 219.

[8] "Dogmatic Constitution on the Church," n. 9, Abbott, p. 26.

[9] "Dogmatic Constitution on the Church," n. 4, Abbott, p. 17.

[10] "Dogmatic Constitution on the Church," n. 7, Abbott, pp. 20–21.

[11] "Dogmatic Constitution on the Church," n. 12, Abbott, p. 30.

[12] "Decree on Ecumenism," n. 2, Abbott, p. 344.

[13] "Dogmatic Constitution on the Church," n. 12, Abbott, p. 30.

[14] "Dogmatic Constitution on the Church," n. 9, Abbott, p. 26.

[15] Ernesto Card. Ruffini, in Congr. Gen. 49, October 16, 1963, *Acta Synodalia Concilii Vaticani II*, vol. II, Pars II (Vatican City, 1972), pp. 629–30.

[16] Léon-Joseph Card. Suenens, "The Charismatic Dimension of the Church" in *Council Speeches of Vatican II*, edited by Y. Congar, H. Küng, D. O'Hanlon (London/New York, 1964), pp. 18–21. It has also been published as an appendix in L-J. Card. Suenens, *Coresponsibility in the Church* (New York, 1968), pp. 214–18.

[17] *Coresponsibility*, p. 214.

[18] *Coresponsibility*, p. 215.

[19] *Coresponsibility*, pp. 216–17.

[20] Yves Congar, O.P., *Lay People in the Church* (London, 1957), chapter 7.

21 Karl Rahner, S.J., *The Dynamic Element in the Church* (Quaest. Disp. 12) (Freiburg/London, 1964), chapter 2.

22 *Acta Synodalia Concilii Vaticani II*, vol. II, Pars III (Vatican City, 1972), pp. 504–5. See also the unpublished Council document: *Schema Constitutionis De Ecclesia*, 1964, pp. 46–47.

23 Above, par. 3, the paragraph beginning with the words: "It is not only through the sacraments."

24 1 Cor 13:3—"If I give away all I have, and if I deliver my body to be burned, but have not love, I gain nothing."

25 "Decree on the Apostolate of the Laity," n. 3, Abbott, pp. 492–93.

26 "Dogmatic Constitution on the Church," n. 30, Abbott, p. 57.

27 "Decree on the Ministry and Life of Priests," n. 9, Abbott, p. 553 (I have slightly revised the translation).

28 "Dogmatic Constitution on the Church," n. 12, Abbott, p. 30.

29 "Decree on the Ministry and Life of Priests," n. 4, Abbott, p. 540.

30 "Decree on the Church's Missionary Activity," n. 23, my translation.

31 George Martin, "Charismatic Renewal and the Church of Tomorrow" in *As the Spirit Leads Us*, edited by Kevin and Dorothy Ranaghan (Paulist Press, Paramus/New York/Toronto, 1971), pp 243–45. (Italics in original.)

32 Kevin Ranaghan, *The Lord, the Spirit and the Church* (Charismatic Renewal Publications, Notre Dame, Ind., 1973), p. 28; also in *New Covenant* 2 (August 1972), pp. 2–3.

33 The First International Leaders' Conference, held at Grottaferrata, Italy, October 9–11, 1973, brought together leaders of such prayer groups from over thirty different countries. It is reliably reported that over one hundred such groups have sprung up in France in the past two years; see Alain Woodrow, "Le Renouveau charismatique, une nouvelle Pentecôte?" in *Informations Catholiques Internationales*, n. 448, January 15, 1974, p. 15.

34 Edward D. O'Connor, C.S.C., "Alienation from the Church" in *The Pentecostal Movement in the Catholic Church* (Notre Dame, Ind., 1971), pp. 239–62.

35 Francis A. Sullivan, S.J., "The Pentecostal Movement" in *Gregorianum* 53 (1972), p. 251; "Baptism in the Holy Spirit: A Catholic Interpretation of the Pentecostal Experience," *Gregorianum* 55 (1974), pp. 60–61.

36 Yves Congar, O.P., "Charismatiques, ou quoi?" in *La Croix*, 19 Janvier, 1974, pp. 10–11.

Liturgy and Charisms

KEVIN M. RANAGHAN

In this article I intend to make some fundamental observations on the charismatic renewal from the viewpoint of liturgical studies. It has not been rare for commentators on the Catholic charismatic renewal to suggest that there is some underlying opposition between the piety and practice of the participants in the charismatic renewal and the authentic spirit of the liturgy.[1] Those who sing exuberantly, pray spontaneously, and testify personally during Penetecostal prayer meetings are said to be reacting against the rational sobriety, the objective structure, and the content of public worship in the Church.[2] These remarks fit well with what until recently has been standard fare from serious students of denominational Pentecostalism. The classical Pentecostals have been said to be anti-liturgical, anti-sacramental, opponents of ritualism, and proponents of completely unstructured, informal, overly emotional, ecstatic, and somewhat mindless gatherings for worship or personal experience.[3]

I would like to suggest in the following pages that the conclusions of liturgical animosity in regard to the Catholic charismatic renewal and indeed in regard to the older Pentecostal movement are ill founded. First, I wish to point out the general nature of denominational Pentecostal worship; its form and content, its distinctive elements, and the ordered pattern in which they occur. We will see that the Pentecostal experience and expression of the Spirit of Jesus as the energizing principle of the worshiping Body of Christ has developed a clear and repeatable pattern of ritual behavior which is at one and the same time the activity which gives the group its corporate identity and that which initiates newcomers into its membership. While recoiling self-consciously from the sacramentalism of other traditions, Pentecostalism has developed its own symbolic and efficacious ritual actions by which the corporate experience of encounter with God is actualized and perpetuated.

In comparison with this picture of denominational Pentecostal liturgy, I wish to examine the experience and practice of the Catholic charismatic renewal. What is the form and content of its worship, and what relationship does it have on one hand to Pentecostal worship and on the other to the Catholic liturgical tradition and renewal? To a significant degree many participants in the Catholic charismatic prayer groups are members of Reformation and even Pentecostal ecclesial communions, with varying degrees of formation in "formal," "liturgical," or "sacramental" churches. However, the overwhelming majority of participants are Roman Catholics, the products of a theological-ecclesial culture marked by heavy emphasis on liturgy and sacramental life. These Catholics have experienced their Church before, during, and after the renewal of Vatican II as a way of life centered upon the Mass and upon Holy Orders as the source of legitimate worship, certain grace, and authoritative teaching. They have known, if with differing levels of understanding, the crucial importance of baptism, the benefit of confession, the consolation of sacramental confirmation, marriage, and anointing. They have been in part refreshed, in part distressed by each phase of liturgical renewal. They have been, whether out of obedience, childlike simplicity, or sophisticated understanding, the children of a mother who transmits life, nourishment, and growth in rituals of worship which signify and effect these necessary goods. They are a people of high liturgical orientation and affinity. This fact has had from the beginning a profound effect on the intellectual presuppositions and the pastoral practice of the Catholic charismatic renewal.

With this in mind we can proceed to examine and compare the processes of ritualization in the Pentecostal churches and in the Catholic charismatic prayer groups. A recently published collection of papers brings together some basic descriptions of ritualization.[4] Margaret Mead has written, "Ritual is concerned with relationships, either between a single individual and the supernatural, or among a group of individuals who share things together. There is something about the sharing and the expectation that makes it ritual."[5] Christopher Crocker puts it this way:

> Ritual is a statement in metaphoric terms about the paradoxes of human existence . . . [it] is essentially communication, a language in which societies discuss a variety of matters. It deals with the relationships a man has to other men, to institutions, spirits, and nature, and with all the various permutations of which these themes are capable . . . Moreover, ritual not only says something; it also does things: it changes one season into another, makes boys become men, transforms ill persons into healthy ones and the ghosts of the dead into the souls of the ancestors.[6]

Finally, we may refer to Aidan Kavanagh's expression of the nature and function of ritualization:

> . . . the patterns of ritual repetitive behavior correspond to and, therefore, may be said to carry, the inchoate and largely incommunicable human experience of reality—for the most part in a non-verbal and always in a parabolic and nondiscursive manner. The whole purpose, as I see it, of assembly, of coming together for public ritual engagements, religious or not, is so that individuals may communicate those experiences that are most incommunicable, publicly, in standard symbolic pattern agreed on by the group so that those experiences can be entered into, "put on," affirmed, and appropriated by the group as a whole. Such standard symbolic patterns are richly ambiguous, but they are also invariably and rigorously judgmental. The point at which the group does, in fact, enter into, finally affirm without reservation, and wholly appropriate the incommunicable life-experiences of its members is that at which judgment falls away in the face of solid affirmation and conviction. It is at this point alone, I submit, that celebration becomes possible if we understand celebration as the single ritual enter-

prise that is subordinated to no further or subsequent ritual pattern.[7]

There are two major ritual events in Pentecostalism and in the Catholic charismatic renewal that I wish to compare and/or contrast. First, the Pentecostal church service with the charismatic prayer meeting; second, the event of Spirit-baptism as it takes place in the Pentecostal churches with its occurrence in the charismatic groups. After detailing both Pentecostal worship and the Pentecostal practice of Spirit-baptism, I will describe the parallel ritual activities in the Catholic charismatic renewal.

In order to present even briefly a typical description of Pentecostal worship, I must make some preliminary observations about the nature and provenance of Pentecostalism. At heart of the Pentecostal churches is a movement of Christian pietism which seeks to involve the believer in the fullness of Christian life through the reception of and perseverance in the central experience of the "baptism in the Holy Spirit."[8] This key experience must be evidenced according to denominational Pentecostals by glossolalia, considered to be speaking in other tongues under the impulse of the Holy Spirit.[9] While the Pentecostal movement had its proper beginnings in the first decade of the twentieth century, it is rooted in eighteenth- and nineteenth-century revivalistic movements.[10] The thrust toward receiving Holy Spirit-baptism was not cut from whole cloth at the beginning of the twentieth century, but was the culmination of a broader religious sentiment which focused upon receiving experiences as the essential element in authentic Christian life. In discussing Pentecostal worship we need to have a clear understanding in context of the use of such words as "crisis," "experience," and "receive." In revivalism generally, and in Pentecostal denominations in particular, the word crisis indicates a time of inner turmoil, questioning, searching, longing, and anxiety on the emotional and psychological levels, and a time of decision and choice on the intellectual and volitional levels. A crisis normally indicates the process or the event by which a person passes from without to within some specific area of Christian living. The word experience is also used with crisis to indicate such a process taking place actually within the life of an individual. The Pentecostal literature regularly describes Christian life as a series of spiritual experiences such as salvation, sanctification, and baptism in the Holy Spirit. Experience indicates a personal assurance, an inner conviction that a particular religious event has, in fact, personally occurred. The word experience is normally limited to those major events in which one is conscious or sure of the presence of God, and of the action of his grace. Experiences are said to be received, and "received" indicates the belief that it is God who is objectively acting in dealing with the individual seeker of the crisis experience. It is God who is actually giving the grace. The word "received" implies the value judgment that the experience is neither self-induced nor the product of outside suggestion, but that it is a reality of grace, in fact, given by God.

The development of Pentecostalism is generally seen to be a movement flowing from the Holiness movement, and American and English Methodism. This history has been seen as one of ideas, principally the theology of sanctification as a second, definite experience of grace subsequent to conversion. However, I am convinced that the lineage from Wesley to the Pentecostals is much more than the handing on of an idea or a theological doctrine. Rather, what has been passed on and developed has been first and foremost a way of worship. One can trace the origin, reoccurrence, and development of certain elements of Pentecostal public worship from their first expression in early Methodism. Through the American colonial and frontier periods, through the frontier revivals and camp meetings, on into the Holiness movement and churches, and finally into the first Pentecostal revivals, these recurrent elements of public worship wend their way into the early development of the Pentecostal movement, and become at last formalized as the elements of denominational Pentecostal public worship.

The principal elements of this worship may be detailed as follows. 1) The expectancy in public worship or common prayer of God's immediate, gracious action resulting in personal religious experiences. 2) A preaching of the Word of God which is emotionally exhortatory, which focuses on the immediate availability of God's grace and which is open to interruption by the congregation in a variety of responses. Such responses are seen to be God's word in and through the members of the assembly. 3) The acceptance and encouragement of congregational participation in the worship service in spontaneous expostulations of praise, in words of encouragement, in personal testimony, in requests for intercessory prayer, in embracing and shaking hands with each other, in the use of glossolalia, in fainting and trances, in dancing, hand clapping, prostration, jumping, and shouting. Throughout the history of the Wesleyan-Holiness-Pentecostal tradition, these elements have grown and developed as the ways in which the members of an assembly participate in worship, especially in response to the immediate presence of the Lord in their midst through his Word and by his Spirit. 4) The development of gospel music, both as a congregational response to the Word and as an exhortatory extension of the Word. 5) The identification of seekers for definite religious experiences, often called mourners (that is, the uninitiated candidates for salvation, sanctification, or Spirit-baptism). These are singled out in preaching and music. They are the objects of intercessory prayer, and much of the congregational participation is structured consciously or unconsciously to have an effect upon the seekers; to move them closer to their reception of the sought-after personal experiences. 6) The development of the altar call and altar service. Originally this was an exhortation to seekers to open, yield, and accept the sought grace by faith. Later, it was coupled with an appeal to step out in faith and come forward from the congregation to an area before the platform and pulpit which was called the altar or mourners' bench or anxious seat. There, publicly identified as seekers, they became the special objects of personal ministry and counseling. The altar and its service has been extended in the development of the prayer room, a place set aside where such seeking and ministry can continue over an extended period of time.

These various elements had previously existed in the Wesleyan and Holiness tradition: in the open-air field preaching, class and band meetings, love feasts, circuit preaching, quarterly meetings, camp meetings, and revivals. At each stage of historical development these elements became more fixed in a ritual pattern of public worship. They became the fabric of liturgy, the shape and content of the central act of public worship, and the heart of Methodist, Holiness, revivalist, and finally Pentecostal culture and society. It was in ritual activity composed of these elements that the crisis experiences were received or at least became publicly acknowledged through testimony. It was in reflection on this worship and in preaching at this worship that the theology of multiple works of grace and experience was developed. It is undeniably true that at each stage of this development there was a withdrawal from certain elements of an older tradition; from a more formal order of service, from the order of the Book of Common Prayer, from the normal Anglican and even more fervent early Methodist practice of Holy Communion, and eventually from the practice of infant baptism. In this sense one may characterize the whole Wesleyan-Holiness-Pentecostal tradition as being anti-sacramental and anti-liturgical. But such a judgment is misleading. What occurred was not the rejection or abandonment of ritual, but the creation and development of new rituals and patterns of worship which more adequately reflected and perpetuated the faith experience of the people involved.

This worship and its constitutive elements have come together and firmed up in the Pentecostal denominations. In the earliest days of the Pentecostal movement (1900–1910) all these elements of worship existed within various Pentecostal assemblies in a spontaneous and unstructured way. As the Pentecostal movement began to develop into various denominations, an order of service which was reminiscent of their previous experience in the Wesleyan-Holiness tradition was substantially readopted. But in the first decade of the Pentecostal movement, such order is only minimally apparent. Looking carefully at the accounts of the Azusa Street revival (1906–1909), we find that elements of the older tradition plus the new emphasis on the spiritual gifts are all present in the revival meetings: tongues and interpretation, prophecy, singing in tongues, spontaneous prayer, testimony, preaching, revivalistic music; all seem to flow together without or-

der or direction. In fact, the role of minister or preacher in these
meetings appears to be clearly subordinate to the leading of the
Holy Spirit as he moves and speaks through the various members
of this Body of Christ. The dynamics of this type of Pentecostal
meeting were largely the result of the arrangement of space in
the meeting room itself.[11] As members of various evangelical and
Holiness churches, the participants in the Azusa revival were familiar with the typical space arrangement of a church building.
Rows of pews where the congregation sat during worship faced a
platform on which a pulpit was most prominent and behind
which various ministers could sit facing the congregation. This
standard pulpit-dominated and therefore preaching- and minister-
dominated arrangement of space was familiar to the earliest Pentecostals. In the denominational period of the Pentecostals there
was a return to this traditional arrangement. By readopting the
layout of the typical Evangelical church, the early Pentecostal
denominational leaders took a step which profoundly affected the
dynamics of congregational worship. But the Azusa revival and
other early Pentecostal meetings broke away from this pattern, if
only for a few years. Influenced by their experiences in small
group, cottage prayer meetings which were the outgrowth of Wesleyan class meetings and love feasts, they sat, not all together facing a pulpit, but rather in a square or in a circle facing each other.
What pulpit there was, was a simple stand before the bench
where the leader of the meeting happened to be sitting. The
leader himself sat on a bench like everyone else, an integral part
of the congregation, and in no way removed or separated from
them. Worshipers sat on a bench or a seat facing each other so
that the Lord and his Holy Spirit might more easily communicate
his living word through what each might share in testimony, exhortation, prophecy, tongues and interpretation.

As the Pentecostal churches emerged from the Pentecostal
movement to become distinct ecclesial communities with their
own buildings and clergy, the free form early Pentecostal meetings began to be shaped into a definite order of service. This
process—slow in some churches, rapid in others—has tended to
regulate the elements of Pentecostal worship. To some degree, the

earlier freedom of congregational participation has been curtailed. In not a few congregations it has almost disappeared. But in the vast majority of American Pentecostal congregations, all or most of the above mentioned elements continue to exist as the shape and content of public worship. Many Pentecostal ministers are reluctant to admit that their services follow a planned order; none of the minister's manuals or service books published by Penetecostal churches in America contains an order of service for congregational worship. But there is an order of service and it is usually admitted upon reflection. From my research I can present the following as typical in its general lines:

1. Opening hymn.
2. Opening prayer of invocation.
3. Extended congregational singing of hymns and choruses with freedom of expression in gesture and movement.
4. Prayers: first by the pastor and then from the congregation; often verbal requests are made for needs; spontaneous testimony to answered prayer may be given; spontaneous prayers of praise and intercession. The congregation may pray aloud together yet individually in English or in tongues. The minister may impose hands on a stack of written prayer requests; prophecy, tongues, and interpretation may occur.
5. Announcements.
6. Tithes and offerings.
7. Special music by the choir, by a group or a soloist.
8. A prayer for the Holy Spirit to anoint the preacher.
9. The sermon, which may well be punctuated by the congregational exclamations of "Amen" and "Hallelujah"; tongues, interpretation, and prophecy often follow the preaching of the Word, extending the ministry of the Word into the congregation where the Word speaks now.
10. Holy Communion on the first Sunday of the month.
11. Congregational singing.
12. The altar call to seekers of personal religious crisis experi-

ence with congregational prayer and music in the background.

13. The altar service in which the seekers meet the minister at
the railing before the pulpit to pray together for the experiences sought; often the ministers will impose hands, altar
workers from the congregation will counsel and pray. The
congregation or part of it may come forward to surround the
seekers with praise and intercession. The choir may sing or
music may be played in the background.

14. Benediction and dismissal which may come during the altar
service, at which time those not at or around the altar rail
may leave.[12]

The Pentecostal service of public worship appears thus as a
miniature revival, a compressed camp meeting. All the elements of
worship combine to express the congregation's belief in 1) the
presence of the risen Christ in the power of his Spirit, 2) the
continual saving action of the Lord among his people through
the ministry of the Word and the spiritual gifts, 3) the saving,
sanctifying, Spirit-baptizing "outpouring" of Christ's grace upon
those who have not yet experienced it. In their expectant faith
and to their present Lord, the congregation responds in spoken
and sung prayer of praise.

While this public worship is the very heart of Pentecostalism,
the event in which the congregation experiences its corporate life
as the Church, it has at the same time an initiatory character. As
heir to the Wesleyan-Holiness religion of revival and experience,
Pentecostal public worship is always oriented toward the initiation of those outside its ambit into the life of Christ and the Spirit.
The preaching, music, use of gifts of tongues, interpretation,
prophecy, and healing, and the demonstrative response of praise
in voice and gesture, while all functions of the inner life of the
congregation, serve also to attract, call, and woo the sinner to
seek the experience of new life in Christ, and call the non-Spirit-
baptized to seek the "latter rain" which the congregation enjoys.
There are, of course, Pentecostal congregations where this does
not happen; where enthusiasm and spontaneity have waned,

and where personal experience has declined. But these instances notwithstanding, I believe that the normal denominational Pentecostal public worship is itself the basic Pentecostal rite or event of initiation.

It is this order of service in general, and the altar service in particular, which provide the ritual context for the key crisis religious experiences of initiation: conversion, sanctification, and baptism in the Holy Spirit. There are variations in the ritual elements depending on which particular experience is focused upon in a particular service of public worship. It is possible, according to the Pentecostals, for these experiences to be received outside of the context of public worship entirely; when one is alone, without any human contact. But, in fact, the denominational order of service itself is geared to bring about these experiences as the climax of public worship. In addition, should someone receive his crisis experience privately, he would be expected to give evidence of it in the congregational setting, either by way of personal testimony or, after private Spirit-baptism, by the use of the gift of tongues in public worship. My focus here is the ritualization of the event of baptism in the Holy Spirit as it takes place in the Pentecostal churches. For the Pentecostals, baptism in the Holy Spirit is a completely distinct experience from that of personal conversion. Though distinct from each other, and most often separated in time, both conversion and Spirit-baptism may be considered part of the overall process of Pentecostal initiation. Spirit-baptism is a personal reception and infilling with the Holy Spirit. While the Spirit does indwell at conversion and is actively present in sanctification, here one experiences being totally immersed or baptized in the Spirit. In conversion, the Spirit baptizes one into Christ; here, Christ baptizes one into the Spirit. This experience is meant for every Christian and without it one is not fully equipped for a mature Christian life. While most Pentecostals would not maintain that it is necessary to salvation, still one's conversion and sanctification are regarded as somehow incomplete without Spirit-baptism. The purpose of Spirit-baptism is the reception of power to be a witness of Christ and power to be a Spirit-led and used member of his body. When one experiences Spirit-baptism, one speaks in tongues and is then able to be used by the Lord in full congregational activity, e.g., giving testimony, prophecy, praying for others at the altar service, praying for healing, using tongues and interpretation, teaching in Sunday school, etc. Spirit-baptism is a definite experience distinct from and subsequent to either conversion or sanctification. It is, therefore, through this experience that one is brought finally into mature Pentecostal denominational life and one's process of initiation is thought to be complete.

From the earliest days of the Pentecostal movement, the event of praying for the baptism in the Holy Spirit was a clearly definable ritual act. Seekers for the experience and those praying with them would come together in earnest prayer to pray for the Holy Spirit to fall upon the seekers as at the first Pentecost. In imitation of apostolic practice, the ministers would lay their hands upon the heads and shoulders of the seekers. All would pray for a short or a long period of time until at last the seekers began to pray in tongues, thereby giving the evidence that they had been filled with the Holy Spirit. This ritual activity occurred spontaneously or upon request, in cottage prayer meetings, in the main meeting room at Azusa Street, or in the prayer room that was set aside for seeking the Holy Spirit. As a Pentecostal order of service began to develop along the lines of the order of the Wesleyan-Holiness tradition, it was logical that this ritual activity should take place as part of the altar call and the altar service at the conclusion of public worship. At some point in the late 1920s and early 1930s, many Pentecostal churches began to abandon the ritual gesture of laying on of hands. All indications are that the Pentecostals became wary of using a rite similar to one used in the formal, sacramental churches. They became wary of any implication of sacramental efficacy through the laying on of hands. The use of this gesture, however, began to reappear and spread rapidly in the Pentecostal churches beginning again in the 1950s. An awareness grew among Pentecostal leaders that the laying on of hands was not only apostolic practice, but that, in fact, people received the Holy Spirit more easily when it was employed.

Today in the Pentecostal denominations, the ritual event of

Spirit-baptism occurs regularly as the climax of a congregational worship service. The worship service itself provides the context for this event; the music, preaching, and exercise of the spiritual gifts in the congregation create in the seekers a desire and expectant faith for the baptism in the Holy Spirit.

The rite may be said to begin with the altar call from the pastor or preacher, challenging and inviting the seekers to come in faith and to receive the Holy Spirit. An appropriate hymn may be played or perhaps sung softly in the background. The congregation begins to pray for the seekers that they will respond and come forward. As each seeker moves forward to the altar rail, he understands it to be a "step in faith"; a declaration of his openness and receptivity. He knows that, as he comes forward, the prayer of the congregation focuses upon him. The altar call may be prolonged in an attempt to reach those who are wavering in their decision to come forward. When those who respond are all in place, kneeling at the altar, the minister in charge usually prays a general prayer for all the seekers that the Holy Spirit may fall upon them, fill them, and that they will speak in tongues. After this prayer, he comes down from the pulpit area and is joined by others from the congregation at the altar to pray with each seeker individually. Meanwhile, a number of the congregation often come forward to stand around and pray for the seekers. The minister or ministers with one or two counselors impose hands on each seeker, praying for him and encouraging him with loud praises to yield to the gift of tongues. As the ministry group moves on to the next seeker, a counselor or one of the bystanders will stay with the one just prayed for, to support and encourage him in yielding to tongues. As each seeker receives tongues, there is a great rejoicing and praise of God. The Spirit-baptism is confirmed. The newly Spirit-baptized is apt to remain praying in tongues for an extended period of time. When he rises, he is embraced by the others and congratulated; welcomed as a "Spirit-filled" brother. Those who do not receive tongues after an extended period of time at the altar are encouraged to "keep on seeking the victory" right then and there, or to come back seeking again another time.

The rite ends as the newly Spirit-baptized and the congregation leave the church, often praising God.

In the preceding pages, we have seen something of the shape and content of denominational, Pentecostal liturgy or public worship composed of a regular repeatable pattern of ritual behavior. These ritual patterns include much spontaneity and freedom. Within its framework, the Spirit is able to move freely among the congregation, to speak and to act through the members of the Body of Christ. It is in these ritual patterns that the Pentecostals experience who they are and share the essential elements of their life in Christ. It is here that they encounter God in the maturity of the worship of the Body of Christ and at the same time incorporate newcomers through the ritual of the altar call into the saved, sanctified, and Spirit-baptized fullness of Pentecostal Christian life. We may now turn our attention to the parallel ritual activity of the Catholic charismatic renewal.

In order to understand the nature of Catholic charismatic prayer meetings, their similarities with denominational Pentecostal worship, and their simultaneous orientation toward the Catholic liturgical tradition, it is helpful to examine the background and origins of the earliest Catholic charismatic prayer groups. The men and women who formed the earliest Catholic charismatic prayer groups in the early months of 1967 were people who were deeply involved in the post-Vatican II work of liturgical, biblical, and ecumenical renewal. Among the earliest participants were a number of theologians, several of whom were specialists in the area of liturgical studies. Likewise, among the students were many young men and women who were dedicated to various activities and projects of spiritual renewal within the Catholic Church. Before the Catholic charismatic renewal began, these people and many who were later to join them, had been experiencing a renewed liturgical spirituality and had been experimenting with a variety of forms of spontaneous and group prayer. From the liturgical movement, with its emphasis on the general priesthood of all baptized believers, and the necessity of full congregational participation in worship, came such experiences as full congregational singing, small group Eucharists, daily praying and singing in small groups, the hours of lauds and vespers, the celebration of Bible vigils, and the extension of the office and Bible vigils into group scripture studies.

Several movements of spirituality which sprang from some of the basic insights of the liturgical movement also made their contribution. For example, a great number of the earliest participants in the Catholic charismatic renewal had been trained in the spirituality of the Cursillo movement. The Cursillo brought with it the practices of small group spontaneous prayer and of small group reunions in which participants spoke freely to each other of their experiences of Christ. At the same time in the mid-60s, a Catholic movement for the formation of spontaneous shared prayer groups with connections to the Anglican Fellowship of Prayer began to appear. Thus, in the years from 1963 to 1967, both at Duquesne University in Pittsburgh, where the Catholic charismatic renewal began, and at Notre Dame University in South Bend, where it was soon to flourish, many of the men and women who were to become the first participants in the Catholic charismatic renewal were engaged in a spirituality which included a high degree of personal participation in the liturgy, spontaneous prayer and sharing in small groups and different types of prayer meetings. When the charismatic prayer meetings began at Duquesne and Notre Dame in 1967, they were not a completely new form of prayer. Spontaneous prayer meetings as such had been going on in these places for some years. What was different about them was the injection of the particularly charismatic elements. While there are certain parallels between these pre-charismatic elements of group prayer and many elements in the Wesleyan-Holiness tradition, one can see that they had their own distinct origin within the developing streams of contemporary Catholic spirituality. Thus, when the first group of Catholics in Pittsburgh who were interested in the baptism in the Holy Spirit attended a Neo-Pentecostal prayer meeting at which Presbyterians, Episcopalians, Methodists, and some denominational Pentecostals were sitting around in a circle in a living room much in the style of the earliest Pentecostal meetings, they did not find the *structure* of the meeting or many elements of the worship particularly foreign to their own practice of group prayer.

The 1974 directory of Catholic charismatic prayer groups lists approximately 3,200 prayer meetings. While some of these prayer groups are quite large with between 500 and 1,000 persons regularly participating, there are in the directory only about 50 prayer groups which report a membership of more than 200 people. The vast majority of Catholic charismatic prayer meetings are smaller; some having as few as 10 members, many more having 50, 75, or 100 participants. While there will be evidence of ritualization in all these prayer meetings, this will be more clearly discernible in the larger groups. In this article, I will attempt to describe the content and structure of worship of a typical Catholic charismatic prayer group of more than 50 members which has been in existence for some period of time and has achieved some degree of stability in terms of the commitment of its members to regular participation, and in terms of its internal organization and leadership. Such a group is composed mostly of Roman Catholic participants. While many such groups may be almost entirely Catholic, it is not unusual for 20 to 40 per cent of the participants in a Catholic charismatic prayer meeting to be members of other Christian churches. Even though such a group might better be termed ecumenical or interdenominational rather than Catholic, the group itself will tend to identify itself as part of the Catholic charismatic renewal in terms of its origin and its ongoing participation in many of the services, publications, and conferences which exist under that name.

The central activity of a typical Catholic charismatic prayer group will be its prayer meeting which most usually is held on a weekly basis. This prayer group is likely to maintain in one form or another a number of ancillary activities, such as: 1) an introductory session in which the basis premises and purposes of the charismatic renewal are explained to newcomers and inquirers, and in which the prayer meeting is outlined; 2) an extensive program of initiation through which those who wish to share in the life of the group come to experience new or renewed life in Christ and the Holy Spirit; 3) a regular course of study for all the members of the group on biblical themes and on the principles and practice of Christian spirituality and the practical problems of Christian living; and 4) a prayer room ministry in which members of the group with spiritual gifts of intercessory prayer, discernment of spirits, and counseling, pray with people with particular spiritual needs, problems, and intentions for themselves or others. Some groups may hold these ancillary activities at a time and place separate from the group's prayer meeting itself. The more common practice, however, seems to be to hold these activities in the hours immediately preceding and following the prayer meeting.

We turn our attention now to the shape and content of the Catholic charismatic prayer meeting itself. The ritual pattern of Catholic charismatic prayer meetings is greatly influenced by and to a great degree determined by the arrangement of space. This arrangement is usually circular. In a small group, this may mean a number of people seated around a living room facing each other. In a somewhat larger group, a number of people might sit on the floor within the circle of seats. As groups get larger, the most common pattern is for rows of chairs to be set up in concentric circles. In all of these examples, the prayer meeting is held with the participants facing the center of the circle and in that way facing each other as much as is possible. It will be noted that this arrangement of space closely parallels the earliest prayer meetings of the Pentecostal movement. Then and now, this arrangement expresses an underlying theology of the Body of Christ and of the place of each member of the Body of Christ in relation to the rest of the group. The group is a manifestation of the Body of Christ. The different members of the group each have their own spiritual gift or service to perform for the benefit of the whole. If there are those with special ministries of leadership, teachers, preachers, prophets, evangelists, those with gifts of healing and miracles, they are not distinguished or separated from the group as a whole, but part of it as members of the congregation. The emphasis here is on the presence of the Lord in the midst of the assembly, leading the group in worship and in spiritual ministry by the power of his Holy Spirit distributed in various gifts among the members of his Body. The action of the risen Lord is here present, immediately available in his worshiping people. The circular arrangement of the prayer meeting argues against a too sharply drawn line between the Christian clergy and the Christian people. It expresses concretely not only the general priesthood of all the faithful participating together in praise and thanksgiving, but also the reality of the diversity of ministries among all the people of God as an important element in the internal structure of the Church.[13] The elements of the prayer meeting and the order in which they occur are certainly not fixed at this stage of development in the Catholic charismatic renewal. One week's prayer meeting may be quite different in content from the next week's. However, the same elements appear with such regularity and are duplicated in most prayer groups to such an extent that one can safely say that a process of ritualization is taking place in the Catholic charismatic prayer groups. In this sense, I can speak of the typical order of a Catholic charismatic prayer meeting:

1. The meeting opens in song led by a group of musicians, usually guitarists, but often including wind, reed, and percussion instruments. During this song, the participants will take their seats and begin to worship in and through the music.

2. A word of introduction from the leader of the meeting. In two or three minutes the leader is apt to welcome everyone, especially newcomers to the meeting, to encourage everyone to enter into the meeting in an atmosphere of faith and worship, to encourage the proper use of the spiritual gifts, and to focus the minds of the participants on the presence of the Lord in the midst of this assembly which is gathered in his name.

3. Throughout the meeting music may be expressed in the following ways: by the leader or any other participants requesting the singing of a particular song or hymn; or by one of the participants simply starting to sing a well-known song or chorus in which he will be joined by the rest of the group; or by the group as a whole beginning to sing using the gift of tongues, as a sung expression of worship, praise, and thanksgiving. All these

types of music regularly occur throughout a typical Catholic charismatic prayer meeting.

4. The spiritual gifts may occur regularly throughout the prayer meeting also. This is true especially of what is called the word gifts: tongues and interpretation, prophecy, testimony, exhortation, scripture reading, teaching, and preaching. These elements interspersed throughout the meeting are often followed by periods of silence or by vocal expressions of praise.

5. Spontaneous prayer is also a regular element of the meeting. It can take the following form: One or more individuals may simply pray out loud spontaneously and in English to the Lord in such a way that their prayer can be heard by the whole group; there may be a litany of praise in which a series of participants will speak out a brief expression of praise and thanksgiving to the Lord, to the Father, the Son, or the Spirit. After each such expression the whole group is apt to praise the Lord together. Another form of spontaneous prayer is the Pentecostal practice of concert prayer, or as it is often called, a "word of prayer" in which the whole prayer meeting prays together out loud at the same time, each one praying his or her own prayer, either in English or using the gift of tongues.

6. Prepared teaching or preaching. Many Catholic charismatic prayer meetings have the practice of including on a regular basis a teaching, testimony, or homily which has been prepared in advance by a chosen speaker.

7. Prayer of petition and intercessory prayer. Throughout the meeting, as a whole, but particularly toward its end, it is common for participants in the prayer meeting to express their particular intentions, needs, and prayer requests for the prayer of the entire group. In smaller meetings each request may be followed by a period of prayer. In larger meetings it is common for all the requests to be mentioned and then to be followed by a general period of prayer. In smaller meetings those with specific needs might be prayed with, receiving the imposition of hands from other members of the group. When there are many requests for personal needs, it is not uncommon for the entire group to

join hands, or to place their hands on each other's shoulders as they spend time in intercessory prayer for all the needs that have been expressed.

In addition to the laying on of hands, a number of other gestures are becoming common in the Catholic charismatic prayer group. While not a universal custom, it is common in many groups for participants to raise their hands in an open gesture of prayer as they praise the Lord together. It is also common for the whole group to stand during part of the prayer meeting in an attitude of praise, and it is not uncommon, particularly in smaller groups and where room permits, for participants to kneel and even prostrate themselves in prayer. Handclapping and rhythmic bodily swaying commonly accompany much of the congregational singing.

The role of the leader varies depending on the size and organization of the prayer group. In groups of all sizes the leader calls the meeting to order, encourages everyone to pray and to use the spiritual gifts at different points throughout the prayer meeting. He may call for periods of silence or encourage periods of more vocal praise. It is his responsibility to maintain order in the prayer meeting, and to calmly take care of any problem or disturbance that might occur. Meetings which have as much freedom and spontaneity as charismatic prayer meetings need to have within them a clearly recognized authority empowered by the group to deal with any occurrence. In the larger prayer meetings the leader needs to function also as an evangelist and as an exhorter. He needs the ability to draw a large group of people together into unity and to lead them in prayer by his example and encouragement. The larger the prayer meeting the more necessary it is for the leader to weave together periods of prayer, silence, music, and openness to the various spiritual gifts. The leaders of prayer groups are most often, although not always, men. Often a group will have two or more leaders who exercise this function one week at a time in rotation.

The typical Catholic charismatic prayer meeting concludes with a final song, perhaps with a series of announcements and some words of encouragement to make use of the surrounding initiation or growth program and the prayer room.

One can easily see that many of the elements in the worship of the prayer meeting are essentially the same as in denominational Pentecostal public worship. At the same time there is in the Catholic charismatic prayer group a sense of relaxation and informality which is not typical in the Pentecostal order of service. It is helpful to point out again that while many of the elements of the meeting, particularly those of an explicitly charismatic nature, have come from Pentecostalism, elements such as spontaneous prayer, sharing, testimony, and congregational singing have their own independent growth in recent Catholic spirituality. The Catholic charismatic prayer meeting seems to mix together elements of worship from these two sources.

While it is possible for the Catholic charismatic prayer meeting to function as an event of initiation, this is not a usual occurrence. In contrast to the Pentecostal order of service, Catholic charismatic prayer meetings do not normally end with an "altar call" or an invitation for newcomers to seek the baptism in the Spirit then and there. This was the practice in the earliest stage of the Catholic Pentecostal movement and may still take place in some smaller prayer meetings. It is, however, being replaced in most prayer groups by a broader program of initiation. The point I want to make is that the Catholic charismatic prayer meeting, in contrast to the denominational Pentecostal meeting, does not have the initiation of newcomers as its regular climax. Rather, the focus of the meeting as a whole is the worship in praise and thanksgiving directed to God the almighty Father through Jesus our risen Lord and Savior through the power of the present Holy Spirit. This worship, praise, and thanksgiving in response to the Word of the Lord shared in scripture and through the spiritual gifts is the purpose for the group gathering together. In itself, then, the Catholic charismatic prayer meeting appears as a whole and complete act of Christian worship in which the assembled group fulfills its purpose by responding in praise and thanksgiving to God's Word and saving action as experienced in the lives of the members. Such an act of worship has its own integral existence and wholeness even though it is not a sacrament and is not normally connected with the celebration of Mass. We must consider, therefore, the nature of preparation for and the ritualization of the initiation process into the Catholic charismatic prayer group, and what relationship this process may have to Catholic sacramental initiation (baptism, confirmation, Eucharist). And finally, we must consider the relationship of the prayer meeting itself to the Catholic liturgy, to the Mass and the sacraments.

Let us turn first to the question of initiation. In the early days of the Catholic charismatic renewal it was common for newcomers who requested it, to be prayed with for the baptism in the Holy Spirit at the conclusion of any prayer meeting. Those who had already received this experience would gather around the seeker and pray with him using the gesture of the laying on of hands. While strongly encouraged, there was not the Pentecostal insistence on the gift of tongues as a proof of Spirit-baptism. In addition to it, prayer groups looked to peace, joy, a new spirit of prayer, and a new awareness of the closeness and the love of Jesus as signs of the Spirit's action. This early practice soon proved inadequate. The number of people coming to prayer meetings who wished to be baptized in the Holy Spirit was growing so large that it was impossible to take care of them adequately at the end of a single meeting. At the same time it became clear that those who prayed for the baptism in the Holy Spirit after a period of instruction, who had time to get their questions answered, and who took time to recommit themselves personally to Christ, often received a more lasting and fruitful experience of grace than those who prayed without such preparation. It became common for many prayer meetings to establish an explanation room, or an explanation session. Those interested in praying for the baptism in the Holy Spirit would be asked to go to this session, either before or after the group's prayer meeting. A talk would be given explaining the baptism in the Holy Spirit as a renewal of the graces of baptism and confirmation and as an empowering to do the work of a mature Christian. After the talk, questions were answered, and then those who desired it were prayed with by a number of people from the prayer group. Soon it became clear that some time between the initial explanation and the actual event of praying for the baptism in the Spirit was helpful. In it seekers could reflect on what they were seeking, could spend some time in prayer and in reading scripture, and generally in drawing closer to the Lord. It became a common practice, then, for people to wait one or two weeks after the explanation session before they were actually prayed with by the group to be baptized in the Holy Spirit. These developments, which took place during the first three years of the Catholic charismatic renewal gave rise to the development of an extensive program of introduction and initiation into charismatic life which is now widely used by a great number of prayer groups. This program is called the Life in the Spirit Seminar and was developed by the Word of God, a charismatic community in Ann Arbor, Michigan. The program which in its published form is presently in its third edition, removes the event of Spirit-baptism from the realm of isolated personal religious experience and places it in the context of a basic explanation of the gospel, of Christian teaching, of conversion to Jesus, of need for the power of the Holy Spirit in successful Christian living. It places the event of Spirit-baptism at the center of an ongoing project of the mature Christian life of prayer, study, service, and involvement in the Christian community.

We cannot treat a person who has been baptized in the Spirit as if he were a fully equipped Christian. He may have all he needs in the Holy Spirit, but he has not yet learned how to relate to the Holy Spirit in such a way that he can receive from the Holy Spirit the needed help.

The Lord was teaching us that we would have to do something more. We would have to introduce people to the Life in the Spirit, and not just "the baptism in the Spirit." We would have to teach them how to begin a consistent relationship with Christ in the power of the Spirit. We learned that if we took the emphasis off the spiritual experience of being baptized in the Spirit and put the emphasis on living a new life in the Spirit, the people would be able to open up to the Lord more successfully and be able to persevere more successfully. We also learned that if we took more time and gave more preparation, more would happen with people. And so we developed the Life in the Spirit Seminars.[14]

Expressed purpose of the Life in the Spirit Seminars is fourfold: 1) to help the persons who come to the seminars to establish or re-establish or deepen a personal relationship with Christ; 2) to help them to yield to the action of the Holy Spirit in their lives so that they can begin to experience his presence and begin to experience him working in them and through them; 3) to help them be joined to Christ more fully by becoming part of a community or a group of Christians with whom they can share their Christian life and from whom they can receive support in that life; and 4) to help them begin to make use of effective means of growth in their relationship with Christ.[15]

The Life in the Spirit Seminar consists of seven catecheses which are given by the leader of the seminar team. The leader is joined by a group of men and women from the prayer group who function as team members. They work in small discussion groups with those making the seminar to counsel with them on an individual basis, and to pray with them during all of the seminars, but especially when they come to the point of committing or recommitting their lives to Christ and of yielding to the action of the Holy Spirit. Here is an outline of the content of the seven catecheses which make up the Life in the Spirit Seminar:

1. God's love. To attract people to the seminar, to dispose them to turn to the Lord, to begin to stir up faith in them.

2. Salvation. To help people see the momentousness of Christianity, to help them understand the basic Christian message (what Jesus has done and will do for them), to help them realize the need to make a serious decision.

3. The new life. To witness to the fact that the Good News is indeed good news, to let the people know that a new life is available through (a fuller) reception of the Holy Spirit, to help them to see that this new life centers in an experiential relationship with the Lord.

4. Receiving God's gift. To help people turn away from every-

thing that is incompatible with the Christian life and to prepare them to act in faith for the full life of the Spirit.

5. Praying for baptism in the Holy Spirit. To help people make an authentic commitment to Christ, to help them to be baptized in the Spirit and speak in tongues.

6. Growth. To help them make a commitment to take the steps they will need to take to insure growth in the life in the Spirit.

7. Transformation in Christ. To help people avoid discouragement over problems they experience, and to help them become part of a charismatic community or prayer group.

The Life in the Spirit Seminars have been constructed so that they might be used equally as well by Catholic, non-Catholic, and interdenominational prayer groups. The authors of the team manual emphasize the need for each prayer group to adapt the seminars to their own particular pastoral needs and problems. The seminars might be presented in one way to a group of nominal Catholics with no experience in the spiritual life and in another way to a group of Catholic clergy, religious, and laity who have been committed to growth in the spiritual life for a number of years. Yet, whether for the first time, or by way of review and renewal, the seminars intend to present at whatever level they are given, a basic Christian catechesis which can lead to and sustain new experience of personal entrance or renewal in vital Christian spiritual life. One can easily see that the originators of the seminars were quite consciously imitating and adapting the pattern of the catechumenate in the early Church. In so doing they are espousing the view that baptism in the Holy Spirit as a personal experience is fundamentally related to the sacraments of initiation in the Church. At the same time they are saying, I believe, that defects in the process and fruitfulness of the sacraments of initiation in the Church are largely traceable to a lack of adequate catechesis in the Church. While the catechumenate in the early Church varied from place to place and time to time in its relation and precise content, it was, nevertheless, the practice to separate the catechumens from the faithful as a separate class of Christians in the process of coming to be, who met regularly for prayer and instruction in the gospel and in the demands and purpose of Christian living. During the catechumenate the catechists regularly prayed with the catechumens, often praying over them prayers of exorcism to free them from the power of the devil seeking to snuff out their incipient Christian lives. The climax of the catechumenate came at last during the celebration of a single liturgy in which the candidates were baptized, received anointing with chrism and the laying on of hands (our present confirmation), and received their first Eucharist. In the weeks that followed their sacramental initiation the newly baptized continued to gather together for instruction in Christian living from the elders of the Church. The structure of the Life in the Spirit Seminars follows this pattern.

One can see in this development the concerted effort to link the contemporary experience of Spirit-baptism and this objective experience of coming into Spirit-filled life in Christ with the objective reality of the graces of Christian initiation conferred in the sacraments of baptism, confirmation, and Eucharist. Thus, to be baptized in the Holy Spirit in the context of the Catholic charismatic renewal in general and the Life in the Spirit Seminars in particular, is not simply to have a strong personal subjective religious experience, a new reception of grace without focus or orientation. It is rather on the subjective level to come into a mature experience of the life of Christ conferred in the sacraments of the Church. The integral relationship between the baptism in the Holy Spirit and the sacraments of Christian initiation has been the most consistent Catholic theological explanation of the baptism in the Holy Spirit since the beginning of the Catholic charismatic renewal.[16] The ritual pattern of praying for the baptism in the Spirit is contained within the fifth session in the Life in the Spirit Seminars. The session begins with some preliminary remarks by the leader explaining that the group will make together a commitment to Christ and that in the time of prayer, there will be both prayers of exorcism and the laying on of hands. The leader also explains how to yield to the gift of tongues and encourages everyone to have the right attitude as the prayer session itself begins. The session itself begins with an opening song and a period of prayer. Then the leader asks the candidates as a group, "Do you renounce Satan and all wrongdoing?" They respond, "Yes." He asks, "Do you believe that Jesus is the son of God, that he died to free us from our sins and that he rose to bring us new life?" "Yes." "Will you follow Jesus as your Lord?" "Yes." Then the leader leads the candidates and all the members of the team in reciting together the following common prayer.

> Lord Jesus Christ, I want to belong to you from now on. I want to be freed from the dominion of darkness and the rule of Satan, and I want to enter into your Kingdom and be part of your people. I will turn away from all wrongdoing, and I will avoid everything that leads me to wrongdoing. I ask you to forgive all the sins that I have committed. I offer my life to you, and I promise to obey you as my Lord. I ask you to baptize me in the Holy Spirit and give me the gift of tongues.[17]

Then those who are praying over the candidate exorcise each one of them and lay hands on them, praying for them to be baptized in the Spirit. They counsel and encourage them as the need arises. The Team Manual suggests that the exorcism should be done simply and undramatically in a quiet voice so that only those who are praying with the particular person may hear it. The team member is advised simply to command whatever spirits are there to depart. Exorcism is described as the traditional word for either casting out evil spirits or telling evil spirits to leave a person or place free. It does not imply that a person is possessed or even obsessed by evil spirits. When everyone is through praying, the leader draws the whole group together. Many of the candidates will probably have yielded to the gift of tongues during this prayer. Therefore, he encourages them to use this gift both in spoken prayer and in song.[18] With minor variations and local adaptations to fit the particular emphasis of different groups, this ritual of praying for the baptism in the Holy Spirit within the context of the Life in the Spirit Seminars is very widely used among the Catholic charismatic prayer groups. Having come through the Life in the Spirit Seminars to a renewed experience of their Christian initiation, the new participants are in a position to rejoin the prayer group in newness of faith and with released capabilities to serve the group and others in the power of the Holy Spirit through a variety of spiritual gifts. Those who have completed the seminars will normally be encouraged to continue their process of Christian education and growth by joining one or more of the growth courses or Bible studies offered by the prayer group.

From observation of the processes of ritualization in the Catholic charismatic prayer groups, we can conclude that in the Catholic charismatic renewal the prayer meeting and the event of Spirit-baptism are separate and distinct from each other, although certainly related. Both the prayer meeting and the initiation process have their independent existence and are not so mutually interdependent that one is incomplete or defective without the other. This contrasts somewhat with the Pentecostal practice in which the act of worship and the ongoing experience of initiation appear to be highly interdependent. In a certain sense one could say that the purpose of the Pentecostal ritual is worship and initiation experience, whereas the purpose of the Catholic charismatic prayer meeting is fulfilled in the perception of the activity of communal worship. We noted above that the Catholic charismatic prayer meetings are complete acts of praise, worship, and thanksgiving even though they are not normally followed by the celebration of Mass. The prayer meeting is, in fact, basically a word service, a type of liturgy of the Word. Normally, this is highly evangelistic in character, not only for newcomers having the effect upon them of calling for repentance and reform of life, but also for the regular members, confronting them over and over again with the demands of the gospel for ongoing repentance and renewal in Christian life.

The prayer meeting is built on the dynamics of all authentic Christian worship. It is the Word of God, Jesus the Lord, who invites participants to gather together in his name in response to his invitation. They give praise and glory to God, then his Word speaks further in the reading of scripture and analogously in the exercise of the spiritual gifts; in prophecy, in testimony, in exhortation, in teaching and preaching. The Word of God works upon the participants in the meeting and leads to resultant acts of even deeper worship, praise, and thanksgiving. Thus the dialogue of Christian worship, the invitation of God's Word, and the response of his people led by the Spirit is complete. In this sense the prayer meetings resemble the celebration of the major hours of the Divine Office in the early centuries of the Church when complete liturgies consisting only of word services were celebrated by monks gathered together in their monastic settlements or by lay ascetics gathered together in cathedral churches or basilicas in the morning, in the evening, or during extended nighttime vigils.[19] One can justly see in the prayer meetings the spontaneous renewal of that spirit of prayer which centered on hearing and responding to the Word of God and which gave birth to the development of the hours of the Divine Office. Those whose concern it is to seek and develop the renewal of the prayer of the Church are to observe carefully what it is that is happening in the charismatic prayer meetings. While many of the elements of these prayer meetings are clearly Pentecostal in origin, the meetings themselves stand squarely in the tradition of Catholic liturgical spirituality based on worship as the work of the people.

Even though the Catholic charismatic prayer meetings are celebrations of worship that are complete in themselves as liturgical celebrations, their liturgical orientation is further demonstrated by those prayer groups which regularly conclude their prayer meetings with a celebration of the Eucharist. While this is not the general practice of Catholic charismatic prayer groups, there are some prayer groups which as a matter of course conclude their meetings with the Eucharist. Some of these groups view the prayer meeting itself as the liturgy of the Word. They then begin the celebration of the Eucharist with the presentation of the gifts.

The charismatic prayer meeting has, in fact, had a profound effect on the celebration of every Eucharist by the participants in such meetings. Their experience of the prayer meeting leads to a more fruitful celebration of the Eucharist through more active participation and a heightened level of subjective faith.[20] When participants in the charismatic renewal celebrate the Eucharist together quite apart from their prayer meeting, they bring to that eucharistic celebration many of the specifically charismatic elements of the prayer meeting. This is particularly true of their use of music, of spontaneous prayer, of the gift of tongues and of other word gifts during the celebration of the Mass. These elements have been inserted into the liturgy without in any way violating the norms for the renewed liturgy. Such a "charismatic Mass" would be marked by very strong and powerful singing at the beginning of the celebration, and a deep and extensive time for reflection and personal repentance. The singing of the Gloria might well be accompanied by singing in tongues or other hymns of praise and of worship. After the oration, the congregation is apt to enter into an extensive word service, including different readings from scripture, prophecies, sharings, and exhortations, leading up to and concluding with the scriptural readings appropriate for the Mass on that day. The eucharistic prayer will be accompanied by the most intense silent devotion and attention which bursts forth powerfully in the singing of the Sanctus, the Acclamation, and the Great Amen. The time after Communion is again marked by the singing of hymns and choruses in English and also by a singing in tongues. It is not uncommon at such a Mass for the final prayer and blessing to be preceded by strong words of prophecy, commissioning the assembly to continue the mission of the Body of Christ as the participants move again from the Eucharist to the world.

This same charismatic character is to be found not only in the eucharistic celebration, but also in the celebration of other sacraments of the Church, most notably at community or prayer group celebrations of the sacraments of matrimony and baptism. It is not uncommon at nuptial Masses to find representatives of the prayer community laying hands on the bride and groom at the prayer of the faithful or at the moment of the nuptial blessing. Nor is it uncommon for many prophecies and words of encouragement to come forward for them at the conclusion of the celebration. But it is perhaps most noticeably in the celebration of the sacrament of baptism that the elements of the charismatic prayer meeting come so powerfully to the surface. It is in the celebration of baptism, the objective gift of new life in Christ, and the bestowal of the Holy Spirit on a new member of the Body of Christ that the charismatic prayer group or community realizes again through the corporate experience of the ritual of the Church the meaning of the gift of the life of Christ and the Holy Spirit. In response to this realization, the liturgy of baptism, which already is so rich in its text and rites, is powerfully supported and celebrated by a community of faith, renewing itself into a commitment to Christ, in yielding to the Spirit, and responding to that in the exercise of the spiritual gifts. Thus, the initiation of the newly baptized becomes a renewal of initiation for the members of the prayer group. And their own personal experiences of Spirit-baptism come into focus in terms of their renewed experience of the sacrament.

One cannot deny that the process of ritualization in the Catholic charismatic renewal is similar to and in many ways dependent upon the process of ritualization in the denominational Pentecostal churches. This in itself can be seen as a genuine contribution of the Pentecostal tradition toward a renewed Catholicism.[21] But on the other hand, one can see that the process of ritualization in the Catholic charismatic renewal is quite different from the process that occurred within Pentecostalism because it is not creating a totally new theological ecclesial culture known as Catholic Pentecostalism. But it is rather in a dynamic and vital way creating new and revitalizing older elements in the Catholic theological ecclesial culture of which it is a part. Those in the Church whose role it is to make celebration more meaningful will have much to learn from charismatic Catholics who view celebration as a way of life.

FOOTNOTES

[1] (Rev.) Henri Nouwen, "A Critical Analysis," *Ave Maria Magazine* (June 3, 1967).

[2] Mary Pappa, "People Having a Good Time Praying," *National Catholic Reporter* (May 17, 1967); "Notre Dame Priests and Students Hold Pentecostal Prayer Meeting," *National Catholic Reporter* (April 19, 1967); "Spiritualists Claim 'Gift of Tongues' at Exorcism Rites," *The Observer* (April 13, 1967).

[3] Nils Bloch-Hoell, *The Pentecostal Movement* (Oslo, 1964), pp. 16, 173ff.

[4] James D. Shaughnessy, ed., *Roots of Ritual* (Grand Rapids, 1973).

[5] Ibid., p. 89.

[6] Ibid., pp. 47–50.

[7] Ibid., pp. 158, 159.

[8] The substance of the following analysis of Pentecostal worship is drawn from Kevin M. Ranaghan, "Rites of Initiation in Representative Pentecostal Churches in the United States, 1901–1972." Unpublished doctoral dissertation, University of Notre Dame, 1974.

[9] Walter J. Hollenweger, *The Pentecostals: The Charismatic Movement in the Churches*, trs. by R. A. Wilson (Minneapolis, 1972), pp. 330–32; G. F. Taylor and L. R. Graham, eds., *Discipline of the Pentecostal Holiness Church*, 5th ed. (Franklin Springs, Ga., 1925); Charles W. Conn, *Like a Mighty Army: Moves the Church of God* (Cleveland, Tenn., 1955); "1916 Statement of Fundamental Truths of the Assemblies of God," cited in Hollenweger, *The Pentecostals*, p. 515.

[10] The best historical work on this development is Vinson Synan, *The Holiness Pentecostal Movement in the United States* (Grand Rapids, 1971).

[11] Frank Bartleman, *What Really Happened at Azusa Street?* (California, 1962).

[12] This outline depends upon my personal research and observation and is a modification of the outline of Frank Masserano, "A Study

of Worship Forms in the Assemblies of God Denomination," unpublished master's thesis (Princeton, 1966), p. 71.

[13] See: "Dogmatic Constitution on the Church," n. 12. I must also point out that there are some large Catholic charismatic prayer groups which have for one reason or another moved their meetings into church buildings and adapted their meetings to the fixed architecture of nave and sanctuary. It is too early to comment upon the effect of this use of space on Catholic charismatic prayer meetings.

[14] *Life in the Spirit Team Manual*, Charismatic Renewal Services, Inc. (Notre Dame, 1973), pp. 5, 6.

[15] Ibid., p. 17.

[16] As early as May 1967 Dorothy Ranaghan is quoted as saying, ". . . she views it as a sort of adult reaffirmation of Baptism and Confirmation." Mary Pappa, "People Having a Good Time Praying," *National Catholic Reporter* (May 17, 1967). See also: Kevin and Dorothy Ranaghan, *Catholic Pentecostals* (Paramus, N.J., 1969); Kevin and Dorothy Ranaghan, eds., *As the Spirit Leads Us* (Paramus, N.J., 1971); Kilian McDonnell, O.S.B., "Statement of the Theological Basis of the Catholic Charismatic Renewal," *One in Christ*, vol. x, No. 2 (1974).

[17] *Life in the Spirit Team Manual*, p. 152.

[18] Ibid., pp. 144–53.

[19] On the early office see: Juan Mateos, S.J., "La vigile cathédrale chez Égérie," *Orientala Christiana Periodica*, XXVII (1961), pp. 281–312; A. van der Mensbrugghe, "Prayer Time in Egyptian Monasticism (320–450)," *Studia Patristica* II (Berlin, 1957), pp. 435–54; I. H. Dalmais, "Origine et constitution de l'office," *La Maison Dieu*, XXI (1950), pp. 21–39; P. Salmon "La prière des heures," *L'Église en Prière*, ed. ed. Edited by A. G. Martimort, et al. (Paris, 1965), pp. 820–31.

[20] This is true of other sacraments as well. See: Michael Scanlon, T.O.R., *Power in Penance* (Notre Dame, 1972); and Francis MacNutt, O.P., *Healing* (Notre Dame, 1974).

[21] "Decree on Ecumenism," n. 3.

Ecumenical Problems and Possibilities

DONALD L. GELPI, S.J.

The piety of Protestant Pentecostals has traditionally focused on the experience of religious conversion. It is a piety rooted in the conviction that Jesus has already fulfilled the conditions necessary for spiritual rebirth. Hence, Protestant Pentecostals in no way doubt that conversion and baptism in the Holy Spirit are free to any man for the asking.[1]

In classical Pentecostal theology, conversion is the act by which one turns from sin and receives the salvation offered men in Jesus. The experience of Spirit-baptism is, however, distinguished from the act of conversion. The vast majority of Protestant Pentecostals tend to equate the experience of Spirit-baptism with glossolalia. Some, however, take the modified view that the tongues experience only inaugurates baptism in the Holy Spirit. Both positions concur in affirming that the experience of the Holy Spirit described in Acts 2 is normative for all Christians. As we shall see, these beliefs are open to serious theological question on more than one count.[2]

Some Protestant Pentecostals recognize a third phase in the process of spiritual transformation: sanctification. Here again, however, there is no creedal uniformity. Some hold that sanctification is instantaneous; others see it as a gradual process of transformation.

It is central to Protestant Pentecostal belief that all of the gifts of the Spirit mentioned by Paul are available to Christians today. Moreover, by comparison with pre-Vatican II Roman Catholic piety, Protestant Pentecostals give the initial impression of being preoccupied with specific gifts: not merely with tongues but with prophecy, healing, and miracles.

Protestant Pentecostal faith-healing has both a psychic and a physical dimension. The religious attitudes of American Protestant Pentecostals are, moreover, colored by the doctrine, popularized by Oral Roberts, that God is never the cause of sickness. There is a concomitant tendency to assign a demonic cause to many physical illnesses, although a distinction is made in principle between ordinary sickness and demonic possession or harassment.[3]

Protestant Pentecostal attitudes toward the sacraments are colored by the doctrines of classical Calvinism. Protestant Pentecostals acknowledge only baptism and the Lord's supper as sacraments. But they look upon baptism as a purely external sign of an inner grace that has already been given. This belief combines with the belief that tongues is the only authentic sign of Spirit-baptism in order to ground the tendency of some Protestant Pentecostals to recommend re-baptism to Christians who receive the gift of tongues subsequent to sacramental baptism.

Protestant Pentecostals tend to look upon the Lord's supper as simply a memorial, a ritual symbol of Jesus' atoning sacrifice which expresses the personal faith of the community assembled in worship. Protestant Pentecostals as a group reject the doctrine of the real presence.

Some Protestant Pentecostals have adopted the practice of foot-washing in obedience to Jn 13:14. But not all acknowledge the practice as obligatory.

The moral attitudes of Protestant Pentecostals as a group, are quite conservative. They acknowledge the Sabbath rest. Some communities practice tithing. Some are convinced pacifists and conscientious objectors. Most oppose smoking and the consumption of alcoholic drinks. Some disallow eating pork. Some oppose playing musical instruments; attending movies, fairs, or theaters; the use of slang; or indulgence in hair-dos, makeup, short skirts, loud clothes, etc. Among Protestant Pentecostals, these tendencies toward rigorism are commonly regarded as a protest against moral laxity and as a protection against religious backsliding.

Protestant Pentecostal piety is often chiliastic in its tone. There is a tendency to insist on an immanent parousia. This otherworldly cast to devotion leaves most Protestant Pentecostals disinclined to engage in active social and political protest or in social reform movements. Many classical Pentecostals regard ecumenism with suspicion.

2. Catholic charismatic piety began as the fusion of traditional Roman Catholic piety with Protestant Pentecostal beliefs and attitudes. Charismatic prayer gatherings are providing most American Catholics with their first extended ecumenical contacts in worship. Ignorance of both Catholic and Protestant Pentecostal doctrine combines with the euphoria generated at prayer meetings in order to blind the less educated Catholic charismatic to the serious doctrinal incompatibilities which still divide him from his Protestant Pentecostal brethren.[4]

Still, the ecumenical significance of charismatic prayer groups should not be underestimated. For there is little hope for the future of ecumenism without a grass roots experience in faith of the common beliefs which unite Christians of different communions.

But if such contact is to bear ecumenical fruit and not syncretistic confusion, both Catholics and Protestants must face in prayer the differences which divide them and begin to seek solutions to their differences.

There is, for example, genuine confusion about the meaning of the term "gift." In medieval Catholic theology, for example, the term "gift of the Holy Spirit" designates the so-called seven gifts. And what Paul calls a "charism," or "gift," is designated in medieval parlance as a "gratuitous grace."

Vatican II, however, marked a major shift in Catholic terminology. In the conciliar documents, the official Catholic pastoral catechesis returned to Pauline terminology. Moreover, post-conciliar Catholic theology has tended to equate the term "gift" with a relatively permanent call of the Spirit to a specific ministry in the Church.

But even this revised Catholic terminology contrasts with the terminology one sometimes encounters among Protestant Pentecostals. Protestant Pentecostal terminology tends not infrequently to contrast "gifts" and "ministries." It thus reserves the term "gift" for speaking of an occasional and striking intervention of the Spirit, an efficacious pneumatic grace which seems to minimize human agency in its visible expression. The term "ministry" designates, then, what contemporary Catholic theologians mean by "gift": a more or less permanent call to service in the community.[5]

How is one to evaluate this tangle of terms? The issues here are more than just semantic because words express and shape religious attitudes.

3. A traditional Catholic theology of the seven gifts of the Holy Spirit is, without doubt, in need of critical re-formulation. The transformation of the seven "spirits" mentioned in Is 11:1–2 into seven formally distinct supernatural "habits" of docility to the Spirit of Jesus is both exegetically and philosophically questionable. A sounder theological approach to the gifts of sanctification would seem to be found in equating the "sanctifying gifts" with that abiding docility to the Spirit which Paul describes as "putting on the mind of Jesus."[6] To such docility, all Christians are called. If abiding docility to the Spirit is legitimately designated as a gift, the term can be legitimately extended to the process by which the Spirit leads the believer to deeper and deeper understanding of the Jesus event and its consequences. A lived understanding of Jesus bears fruit, however, in one's being set apart by God for himself, i.e., in the process of sanctification. The Spirit's call to sanctification is, then, experientially like his call to service and can, therefore, be understood under the rubric of "gift." What distinguishes the call to sanctification from the service gifts is the universal character of the call to sanctification. All believers are called to "put on the mind of Jesus." But, while all are called to some kind of service, not all receive the same service gift.

The restriction of the term "gift" to an occasional, extraordinary intervention of the Spirit, however, seem to be exegetically indefensible; for it binds the term to the occasional and to the extraordinary. In speaking of the "charisms" of the Spirit, however, Paul applies the term to many activities that can only be interpreted as permanent and pedestrian: marriage, the apostolate, official office, administration, helping.[7]

The term "gift" would, then, seem to be best restricted in the first instance to the more or less permanent calls to service within the community which the Spirit gives. But it may be extended by analogy to the permanent call of the Spirit to every Christian to put on the mind of Jesus.

As we have already suggested, these problems are more than just semantic. Traditional Catholic restriction of the term "gift" to the *sacrum septinarium* is symptomatic of the alienation of pre-Vatican II Catholic charismatic theology from biblical patterns of thought. It is also symptomatic of an unfortunate tendency in medieval Catholic theology to disassociate service to the community from the process of personal sanctification. A sounder approach would seem to be to regard the service gifts as providing the ecclesial context within which an individual is to work out his personal sanctification.

The Protestant tendency to restrict the term "gift" to the more extraordinary occasional manifestations of the Spirit is symptomatic of an unfortunate tendency to disassociate the gifts of the Spirit from the institutional expressions of religion. It also suggests that tendency to become preoccupied with the more extraordinary manifestations of the Spirit against which Vatican II warned.

4. But the theological issues dividing Catholic charismatics and Protestant Pentecostals go much deeper than terminology. There would seem at present to be no way of completely reconciling a Catholic and a classical Protestant Pentecostal account of Spirit-baptism, although, as we shall see, a Catholic theology of confirmation and a Protestant Pentecostal theory of "second blessing" have a certain affinity and might provide an opening for a fruitful ecumenical exchange.

The classical Pentecostal disassociation of conversion from Spirit-baptism would seem to reduce conversion to a purely human process. Such a doctrine has, however, a Pelagian or Semi-Pelagian ring.

In Catholic theology an adult cannot repent authentically and turn to God without receiving the Spirit. Baptism of blood and of desire both mediate saving grace, the divine indwelling. Moreover, in Catholic sacramental theology, an infant can receive the

Spirit prior to personal conversion. All of these Catholic doctrines would seem to be theologically non-negotiable, although Catholic theologians engaged in ecumenical dialogue with Protestant Pentecostals would do well to seek a re-formulation of them that is less offensive to pious Protestant ears.

The classical Pentecostal attempt to invoke tongues as the sole criterion for the reception of the Spirit is also unacceptable from the standpoint of Catholic doctrine. There is no evidence in scripture that all who received the Spirit received tongues, not even on Pentecost day. There is clear evidence in scripture that some of those who did receive the Spirit did not speak in tongues.[8]

From the standpoint of Catholic doctrine, to regard tongues as the only decisive sign of the reception of the Spirit is, moreover, elitist and divisive in its consequences. For in canonizing a specific service gift as the only decisive sign of the Spirit, one calls into question the ecclesial status of any member of the community who does not possess that specific gift. One might as well say that only prophets are Spirit-baptized, or that only administrators are.

Since, however, this classical Pentecostal belief is largely rooted in a fundamentalistic reading of Acts 2, it seems unlikely that those who espouse it will be able to modify their views without coming to terms with the inadequacy of the fundamentalistic methodological presuppositions which ground their approach to scripture. The abandonment of fundamentalism is, however, no small matter. It demands a major intellectual conversion and the critical re-evaluation of a host of intellectual, moral, and emotional attitudes which the fundamentalist, for a variety of personal reasons, is unwilling to face. Needless to say, however, Protestant Pentecostals have no corner on fundamentalism. The manual tradition in Catholic theology, which has formed the religious attitudes of generations of lay and clerical Catholics, is as fundamentalistic in its presuppositions as many a Protestant. Moreover, fundamentalism, whether Catholic or Protestant, remains the most serious obstacle to meaningful Catholic-Pentecostal dialogue.

Although a Catholic and a classical Pentecostal account of conversion would seem to be at loggerheads on most points, they would appear to converge, without quite meeting, when it comes to the notion of a "second blessing" granted to the believer after his initial conversion.

Traditional Catholic theology of confirmation holds that in this sacrament there is a "second sending" of the Spirit over and above his mission in baptism. In what does such a second sending consist?

As St. Thomas has suggested, the sending of a divine peron is best understood as the visible, salvific transformation of men.[9] In baptism one is transformed by reception of the Spirit "invisibly" but personally. The visible transformation of the believer is effected initially by the gifts of sanctification, the basic grace of baptism. If, therefore, one is willing to acknowledge a distinction in relationship between such an initial transformation of the believer and that mediated by the reception of a specific service gift, then the reception of the service gift can be legitimately described as a "second sending" of the Holy Spirit over and above his sending in baptism. On this analysis, the reception of some service gift or gifts would constitute the chief grace of confirmation.

The tendency in some Protestant Pentecostal circles to disassociate sanctification from conversion and from the "second blessing" is also unacceptable from the standpoint of Catholic theology. For Catholics, "sanctification" designates the total process by which one is transformed in the image of Jesus. It includes the "invisible" sending of the Spirit in baptism and culminates in the believer's final transformation into glory.

5. The popular Pentecostal belief that God wills the physical healing of all men is another source of confusion in some Catholic prayer groups. The problem with this doctrine is that it is simplistic. It fails to distinguish adequately kinds and degrees of healing.

There is a very real sense in which conversion itself is a healing. It heals human sinfulness and alienation from God. The transformation of physical suffering into a grace is also a kind of healing. It occurs when physical sickness ceases to be an experience of misery and suffering alone and becomes instead an experience of deepened faith-dependence on God.

Physical healing is salvifically justified when it leads to deeper conversion and faith. When there seemed to be no hope of effecting such a salvific effect, Jesus is portrayed in scripture as being reluctant to heal.[10]

Sickness can, moreover, confront the unbeliever with his own limitations and need for salvation. If in certain cases the unbeliever can come to God in no other way, it seems unlikely that God would refuse such a person the grace of illness.

Sin alone is absolutely evil. Sickness can function in experience as a sign of man's alienation from God and need for salvation, especially when it is endured without faith. But sickness is salvifically indifferent, for it can be transformed into a grace.

Moreover, the belief that sickness can never be attributed to divine agency and is quite possibly demonic in origin leads to consequences that give indications of being from some source other than the Spirit who is the bond of union. It not infrequently motivates judgmental attitudes toward those who pray for physical healing without receiving it. To tell such persons that the only explanation for their continuing suffering is that they lack faith or are harassed by demons is not only irresponsible but runs the serious risk of blinding the sick to the kind of healing which God desires to give them.

6. The most serious doctrinal differences dividing Catholic charismatics and Protestant Pentecostals lie in the area of sacramental theology. The theological deficiencies lie on both sides. Catholic theology has largely ignored the gifts for centuries, although it is in process of rediscovering them.[11] As a result Catholic sacramentology shows little or no consciousness of the intimate relation which exists between the gifts and the sacraments.

Protestant Pentecostal theology has for its part tended to substitute for serious reflection on the meaning of the sacraments an unthinking acquiescence in the polemic rhetoric of classical Calvinism.

It is, however, possible to demonstrate through a foundational theological analysis that the sacramental system is unintelligible unless it is grounded in a theology of gift and that the gifts of the

Spirit are unintelligible if they are divorced from their sacramental expression.

More specifically, it is possible to demonstrate that the gifts of sanctification in the sense redefined above are the chief grace of baptism, that the service gifts are the basic grace of confirmation, that marriage and orders are sacraments because they are rooted in service gifts, that confession and the anointing of the sick are rooted in the gift of healing and that the total pragmatic effectiveness of the Eucharist presupposes its celebration in a community that is open to all the service gifts.

I am at present preparing a detailed exposition of these ideas, but the argument is too intricate to summarize here.

It suffices here to note that both Catholics and Protestant Pentecostals have a lot of rethinking to do on these questions. Until that rethinking is done, the imposition of the sacramental practices of either group's communion on the other smacks of serious pastoral irresponsibility. I am referring specifically to Protestants who urge Catholics to be rebaptized after they receive the gift of tongues and of Catholics who press for open eucharistic communion before the proper ecumenical, pastoral, and doctrinal foundations have been laid for open communion.

Protestant Pentecostals who hold that the Eucharist is only a memorial would do well to reflect on the difference between recalling a telephone number and recalling God's saving action in the power and anointing of his Spirit. If they are willing to do so, they will be on their way to a theologically sound understanding of why Catholics believe in the real eucharistic presence. Catholics for their part are often in need of updating their own understanding of sacramental presence in categories that are more directly experiential and less tied to antequated philosophical positions.

7. In what touches the ethical stance of Protestant Pentecostals two points need to be made.

First, it seems unlikely that Protestant Pentecostals will ever convince the mass of Roman Catholics to adopt the rigoristically tinged attitudes they espouse in smoking, drinking, dress, etc.

There are Catholic rigorists, of course. But Catholic piety has still a greater affinity to Latin tolerance in such matters than to Germanic austerity. Though Catholics may in many instances do well to re-examine their own attitudes on some of these questions, for the present a live-and-let-live attitude which allows for degrees and styles in personal austerity would seem to be the best working solution.

A more serious problem is, however, posed by the tendency of Catholic charismatics to absorb the otherworldliness of classical Protestant Pentecostal piety. It is a basic trait of Christian piety that one desire that the coming of Christ be soon. But it is one thing to desire the coming of the Lord and another to start setting timetables. And it is still another thing to use one's hope for the arrival of the Lord as a fallacious excuse to neglect the plight of the destitute and the socially and politically oppressed. Nor can one look with equanimity on the ease with which a number of Catholic charismatics have absorbed the exegetical confusions of a book like *The Late, Great Planet Earth.* Perhaps popular folk religion will always manifest such tendencies; but it is pastorally irresponsible to allow them to develop without challenge.[12]

At the heart of these tendencies in Protestant Pentecostal piety is a much deeper set of attitudes: fundamentalism. There are, of course, fundamentals to the Christian faith in the sense that there are specific realities and ideals to which one must be committed in order to be intelligibly designated as a Christian. But the fundamentalist's grasp of such fundamentals is marred by two untenable sets of presuppositions. The first is the absence of what Bernard Lonergan has called "intellectual conversion." The fundamentalist is a person who is lost in the myth of "the given." He naïvely believes that truth can be simply handed to him objectively on a platter. As a consequence in approaching the sources of revelation he attempts to resolve the truth or falsity of a proposition of faith before he has attempted to resolve the more basic question of the meaning that that proposition had for the one who wrote it. Believing truth to be "objectively there," he assumes that what he believes to be true is what every other true believer holds. When such attitudes are combined with the subjectivistic tendencies present in "inner light" piety, they tend to produce a divisive brand of doctrinal Gnosticism: the tendency to endow one's personal biases and prejudices with self-evident truth-claims that are binding on all believers.

More serious still is the tendency of some forms of charismatic rhetoric to divorce faith commitment to Jesus from commitment to active social reform. In principle there need be no such divorce. But the indications are that it in fact exists in more than one place. Such tendencies would seem to be traceable to the more basic tendency in revivalist piety to describe faith in Jesus as bringing assurance of one's personal salvation rather as the mature assumption of personal responsibility in the Spirit for the moral and social consequences of commitment to God and to men in the image of Jesus. Catholic charismatics must realize that their continued abstention from active participation in movements of social reform can only continue to render charismatic piety suspect in the eyes of their fellow Catholics.

8. Paul counsels the Christian community and its leaders to test all things and hold on to those spiritual impulses which are good. It should be clear from the preceding reflections that not all the impulses in the Catholic charismatic renewal can meet the Pauline test, although many, many impulses can. I state this as one actively involved in the renewal and convinced that it is on the whole the work of God. But no religious revival has ever been free of foibles, and the Catholic charismatic renewal is no exception.

Not all of the foibles of the renewal are traceable to ecumenical contact. Many are bred of inauthenticities in the American Roman Catholic tradition. But it is clear that to some degree premature ecumenical contacts have fostered fundamentalist tendencies among Catholic charismatics and the uncritical absorption of the more questionable philosophical presuppositions which ground fundamentalist piety. Until adequate pastoral instruction and decisive leadership has effected the correction of such problems, to press ahead where they exist with an extension of ecumenical contacts would seem to be seriously ill advised.

The world of ecumenism is a china closet. It does not need bullheaded people. At the present juncture, enthusiasm for the fruits of carefully supervised ecumenical contacts in major centers for the charismatic renewal could produce an unfortunate blindness to the pastoral confusions which are being bred of premature ecumenical contacts away from these major centers.

It is, of course, all but impossible to generalize in such matters. The charismatic renewal gives evidence of being able to effect a deep spiritual renewal among Catholics. It has already served as the means for the kinds of shared ecumenical prayer experiences which are indispensable to healing the divisions which exist among Christians. Everyone desires that such contacts will continue and deepen. But they will not do so without a deepening of repentance on the part of Catholics and Protestants both, a repentance which leads to a unifying transformation of both communions. For the problems raised in this article are real ones. And they will not be resolved by prayer alone; nor will they be resolved by pretending that they do not exist. They will be resolved by professional, Spirit-led theological reflection and by a deeper conversion on the part of Catholics and Protestant Pentecostals at an affective, intellectual, moral, and religious level. For it is only in conversion to God that we open our hearts to the guidance and healing of the Spirit.

FOOTNOTES

[1] For a thoroughly documented and sympathetic assessment of the traits of Protestant Pentecostalism developed in this essay, see: Walter Hollenweger, *The Pentecostals: The Charismatic Movement in the Churches* (Augsburg, Minneapolis, 1972); see also John A. Hardon, S.J., *Protestant Churches of America* (Image, New York, 1969), pp. 169–83.

[2] Two of the more recent critiques of the Protestant Pentecostal theory of conversion are: Frederick Dale Brunner, *A Theology of the Holy Spirit* (Hodder and Stoughton, London, 1971); James Dunn, *Baptism in the Holy Spirit* (A. R. Allenson, Naperville, Ill., 1970). For a non-fundamentalistic reading of Acts 2, see: George T. Montague, S.M., "Baptism in the Holy Spirit and Speaking in Tongues," *Theology Digest*, XXI (Winter 1973), pp. 342–60. See also: Simon Tugwell, O.P., "Reflections on the Pentecostal Doctrine of 'Baptism in the Holy Spirit,'" *Heythrop Journal* (1972), pp. 402–14; Robert Wild, "Baptism in the Holy Spirit," *Cross and Crown*, XXV (June 1973), pp. 147–61.

[3] For a sympathetic approach to the theology of faith-healing, see: Morton Kelsey, *Healing and Christianity* (Harper and Row, New York, 1973); Donald Gelpi, S.J., "The Ministry of Healing" in *Pentecostal Piety* (Paulist, New York, 1972), pp. 159–62.

[4] Cf. Edward O'Connor, C.S.C., *The Pentecostal Movement in the Catholic Church* (Ave Maria, Notre Dame, 1971); Kilian McDonnell, O.S.B., "Catholic Pentecostalism: Problems in Evaluation," *Dialogue*, IX (Winter 1970), pp. 35–54; Stephen Clark, *Where Are We Headed?* (Charismatic Renewal Services, Notre Dame, 1973); Kenneth Peters, "Six Surprising Years: Catholic Pentecostals," *Today's Parish* (September–October 1972), pp. 6–8.

[5] For a devout and sensitive meditation on the Thomistic "seven gifts," see M. M. Philipon, O.P., *Les Dons du Saint-Esprit* (Desclée, Paris, 1963). For a sample of pre-Vatican II theology of the

gifts, see: Karl Rahner, S.J., *The Dynamic Element in the Church* (Herder and Herder, New York, 1964); Yves Congar, O.P., "The Church and Pentecost" and "The Holy Spirit and the Apostolic Body, Continuations of the Work of Christ" in *The Mystery of the Church* (Helicon, Baltimore, 1960). For the impact of Vatican II on the theology of the gifts, see: Gabriel Murphy, *Charisms and Church Renewal* (Catholic Book Agency, Rome, 1965). See also: Arnold Bittlinger, *Gifts and Graces*, translated by Herbert Klassen (Hodder and Stoughton, London, 1967); Josephine M. Ford, *Ministries and Fruits of the Holy Spirit* (Catholic Action Service, Notre Dame, 1973).

[6] Phil 2:5; I Cor 3:16–17.

[7] I Cor 13:28; Eph 4:11.

[8] I Cor 12:30.

[9] *Summa Theologica*, I, Q. 43.

[10] Mt 6:6.

[11] For a fine foundational analysis of the relation of the Spirit to the sacramental system, see: Joseph M. Powers, S.J., *Spirit and Sacrament* (New Seabury, New York, 1973). For a sample of more recent approaches to the charisms, see: Hans Küng, S.J., *The Church* (Sheed and Ward, New York, 1969), pp. 150–260; *Why Priests?* (Collins, New York, 1972); Gotthold Hasenhüttl, *Charisma, Ordnungsprinzip der Kirche* (Herder, Freiburg, 1969); William Koupal, "Charism: A Relational Concept," *Worship*, XLII (November 1968), pp. 539–45.

[12] Cf. Joseph H. Fichter, S.J., "Pentecostals: Comfort vs. Awareness," *America* (September 1, 1973), pp. 114–16.